YOUR CHILD
IN SCHOOL

Tom and Harriet Sobol

YOUR CHILD IN SCHOOL

*Kindergarten Through
Second Grade*

Arbor House • New York

Manufactured in the United States of America

10 9 8 7 6 5 4 3 2 1

Library of Congress Cataloging in Publication Data

Sobol, Tom.
  Your child in school.

    1. Kindergarten.   2. First grade (Education)
3. Second grade (Education)   4. Home and school.
I. Sobol, Harriet Langsam.   II. Title.
LB1169.S63   1987   372'.21   86-20652
ISBN: 0-87795-867-X

This book is dedicated to your child in school,
And to our children,
Sandy, Tom, Michael, Greg, Jenny, and Jeffrey,
From each of whom we learn so much

Contents

Acknowledgments

The idea for this book was originated by Edward A. Shergalis, Jr. Without him we would not have undertaken this project.

Michael Cohn, Alan Jaffe, and James Raimes provided competent technical advice and welcome moral support.

Many teachers and parents gave generously of their time and knowledge. We thank them all, and especially Ellen Anders, Margaret Bartelme, Lila Berger, Ardis Burst, Leda Canino, Ellen Citron, Marlene Cohen, Adele Fiderer, Joanne Glassner, Victor J. Goldberg, Selma Grossman, Judy Harary, Howard Harrison, Ann Hirsch, Ethel Huttar, Liz Jaffe, Tema Kaufman, Marge Lewis, Joan McCann, Don Monroe, Mary Murillo, John Plummer, Gladys Redhead, Maj-Britt Rosenbaum, Itamar Salamon, Ann Schaeffer, Marjorie Schlosberg, Lora Shepard, Ruth Silverman, Flo Sinsheimer, Judy Sondheim, Jo Sopis, Ann Spindel, Dick Sprague, Paula Sternberg, Janet Thomas, Barbara Wallach, Grace Zuckerman, the staff of the Scarsdale Public Library, the friends who listened, and the front hall still waiting to be fixed.

The Authors

Preface

Your child's most impressionable years will be spent in school. From the time he leaves your side to enter kindergarten until the high school graduation ceremony thirteen years later, your child's waking life will be shaped by events at the schoolhouse. In the classroom and on the playground, on the school bus and in the crowded corridors, children make their own friends, discover their talents, struggle with their problems, find their place. They learn the folklore and the norms of our culture, and, if all goes well, they develop the skills and acquire the knowledge to become successful in the world beyond the school.

But how do you, as a parent, know how well the process is going? How do you know whether what is happening at school is what is supposed to be happening? What do children and teachers *do* at school, all day long, day after day? How do you know if the teachers are doing the right things, and how do you know if your child is making normal progress? And if your child is not making normal progress, when should you worry, and what should you do about it?

The authors have felt enough pride and enough pain of their own to know that parents of children in school occasionally need help. Between us, we have raised six children, of widely differing abilities and interests and temperaments and limitations. Each one's school experience was different. Each required fresh insight, new understanding, held breath, sustained humility. We thank the few wise and capable people who helped us through; we hope we can repay our debt to them by helping you.

Finally, a word about school people and the school itself. Between us, we have taught children in elementary school, adolescents in junior and senior high school, young adults in college and graduate school, and older people in adult-education classes. We have talked with our students' parents and friends, and we have supervised teachers at all levels. We have attended and worked in school in the favored suburbs and in the inner cities. And as superintendent of schools, one author has spent meeting after meeting, year after year, helping parents deal with their anxieties about their children.

Out of this experience we have come to have deep respect for the curious institution called the school. For all its sad shortcomings, it is one of the few places in our society where people get together and try to become more than they are. School may not always be the best place for learning, but as Robert Frost said of love and the earth, we don't know where it's likely to go better.

How to Use This Book

This book has five main parts: "The Primary Child as a Learner," "Kindergarten," "First Grade," "Second Grade," and "The Primary Years." The first part concerns the way in which young children develop mentally. The three middle parts describe the branches of the curriculum and common instructional practices grade level by grade level. The part "The Primary Years" deals with general matters, like tests and learning problems, which are not specific to a given grade level.

Some readers may wish to read straight through from beginning to end. That, after all, is how your child will do it—from September of the kindergarten year to June of the second grade. If you read the book in this fashion you will gain a sense of what your child's experience in school will be, in both its continuing freshness and its regularity and repetition.

Other readers may wish to refer to those sections or topics of particular importance to them. For that reason we have tried to include relevant information on each topic at each grade level. This approach requires occasional repetition. In the second grade, for example, the teaching of reading is not fundamentally different from that in the first. Teachers build on what children have learned in the first grade, but because children learn at different rates, most of what is taught in first-grade classrooms appears in second-grade classrooms as well. Rather than refer the reader to the "First Grade" section, we have restated the first-grade material in somewhat abbreviated form in the "Second Grade" section. We hope the reader will pardon the redundancy, which mirrors the experience your child will have in school.

If you do use this book as a resource on specific topics or a specific grade level, we urge you always to read a little before and a little after the section you have chosen. Life in schools is not as neatly compartmentalized as a table of contents suggests.

Finally, a word about the "he/she" problem. The English language has not yet made up its mind about the niceties of non-sexist locution. When we began writing, we said "he or she" until we could stand the awkwardness no longer. Then we varied pronouns—sometimes "he," sometimes "she"—until we couldn't remember which sex we were using. Eventually we gave up and said "he" for the child and "she" for the teacher, the latter on the factual ground that more elementary teachers are female than male. Needless to say, we mean all children and all teachers, regardless of gender.

THE
PRIMARY CHILD
AS A LEARNER

"All men by nature desire to know."

So said Aristotle, and so says anyone who has lived or worked with young children. Children of primary-school age are insatiably curious, wonderfully adaptive, eager to learn the ways of their parents and teachers. So strong is their natural instinct to learn that it is all but impossible for the teacher to spoil it. Unfortunately, some few succeed in doing so. In most children, however, the drive to learn is so strong that success in the early years of school is almost assured. A knowledgeable parent and a sensitive teacher can guide children's learning activity so that it becomes even more productive. But young children continue learning even in mediocre settings. Parents should approach the first years of school with confidence, ready to help but secure in the miraculous power of the children to whom they have given life.

Consider what children have learned before they enter school. They are born with an instinct to suck, an instinct to grasp, a drive to live and to learn. Within four or five years, usually without benefit of schooling, they have mastered some of the most important and difficult lessons of their lifetime. They know the difference between self and others, between family and strangers. They grasp the connection between cause and effect. They have a developing sense of time—of past, present, and future. They understand and can express spatial relations—up from down, in from out, front from back. They can use the grammar of their language, and they have a burgeoning vocabulary.

These are tremendous achievements, and the drive to continue building on them carries on into the early school years.

JEAN PIAGET

One of the world's most respected writers about young children as learners is the Swiss psychologist Jean Piaget. Piaget and his followers studied children's mental growth closely from infancy through childhood and proposed a theory of development based upon their observations. According to Piaget, all children tend to see the world in the same general way, and they proceed more or less uniformly through a series of fixed stages of increasing complexity.

From birth to one and a half or two years, the child is in the *sensory-motor* stage. At this stage the child's intelligence develops through physical manipulation of his immediate environment. His concern is focused on the mastery of objects—toys, blocks, pots and pans, rocks. Gradually, the child develops a sense of *object constancy* (that people and things exist even when he can't see them), a primitive sense of cause and effect, and a rough sense of time.

From about two to seven years of age, the child is in the *preoperational* stage. At this stage, children increasingly learn to substitute language and mental images for the direct physical groping of infancy. Through play and make-believe, they imitate the ways of the adults in their lives, and in their minds they create pictures of the world beyond their immediate senses, though the pictures may often be inaccurate from an adult's point of view. (For example, a child may believe that the moon rises only for him and that it follows him down the street.)

From about seven to eleven or twelve years of age, the child is in the stage of *concrete operations*. In this stage, children can think about objects and actions without perceiving or performing them. They understand numbers and relationships. They can project things into the past or future and imagine things in new combinations. They can also communicate more easily as their power of language continues to grow. However, their thought remains closely tied to their actual concrete experience. They are not yet ready to think about abstractions that transcend physical reality as they have known it.

At about eleven to twelve years of age, the child enters the stage of *formal operations*. In this stage, normally the time of early adolescence, children can think about abstract ideas as well as about things. They can entertain hypotheses, construct mental models, discover general laws that underlie discrete phenomena. Their intellectual functioning, although not necessarily their knowledge or their wisdom, is fully mature.

Many educators in the United States espouse Piaget's theory, and those who do not are heavily influenced by it. What implications does it have for your child in the primary years?

- Since children in the pre-operational stage see the world differently from adults, the child's mind must be respected. Constantly telling children that they are "wrong" is not helpful. Good teachers engage children at the children's level of mental maturity, and through questioning and guidance lead them to clearer understanding.
- Since children's thinking is closely tied to concrete objects and experience, the child must learn by doing. Telling is not teaching. As Piaget says, true knowledge is a construction from within. Children derive meaning from their own personal experience. Good teachers involve children with interesting materials and activities and help them explore the possibilities of these materials and activities.
- Since children make sense of their world through make-believe and play, much of their learning activity should resemble play. As the old saying goes, the work of the child is play.
- Since children develop mentally through a series of fixed stages, they must be allowed the time required for growth. Quality of mental activity, rather than speed of development, should be emphasized.
- Since children learn from their direct experience in the here and now, the chief goal of the primary program should be to nurture children's mental activity. The goal is not to master rigid curricula or a fixed body of knowledge. Experiences that reward curiosity, thought, imagination—these are the rich stuff of the primary program.

The authors believe that these ideas, supported by Piaget's theory, make substantial sense. However, your child's primary teacher need not be a learned disciple of Piaget to be effective. All that is required is a respect for the child's mind, a willingness to engage that mind on its own terms, and an ample supply of loving patience. Out of such engagement, the child will continue to unfold the miracle of human learning.

INDIVIDUAL DIFFERENCES

However true Piaget's stages may be as a model of all children's mental development, they cannot possibly predict with accuracy the course of your own child's development. Children vary widely in their rates of physical, mental, and emotional growth, and the differences are especially pronounced at this age level.

In the pages ahead you will discover how teachers go about guiding your child's development and learn what the signs of normal progress are. But both you and the teacher should always remember that you are dealing with an individual: a unique person with his own capacities, experiences, and timetable for growth—your child. In the authors' view, there is no such thing as the average child. Each child is special, especially yours. We hope these pages will help you find your child's special qualities and nurture them as he becomes more fully human.

KINDERGARTEN

The Kindergarten Child as a Learner

What learning qualities do children of kindergarten age display? Typically, kindergarten children are

- *Curious* about the world around them. They are eager to explore everything in their physical environment, open to new experiences, intrigued by words and letters and numbers and keyboards and computer screens. They want to use their senses, their hands, their minds.
- *Active* in pursuing their curiosity. Kindergarten children are a cluster of verbs: talking, listening, playing, touching, tasting, smelling, cutting, pasting, measuring, constructing, trying, questioning. They move almost constantly and need frequent changes of activity in keeping with their short attention span.
- *Eager to please adults.* They wish to please their parents most of all, but they usually transfer dependence to their teacher as well. The kindergarten teacher must be very grouchy indeed if your child doesn't like her. Never again will children be so ready to respond to adult wishes.
- *Imitative* of adult behavior. Sometimes the imitation is obvious, as when children play at adult roles—being the teacher, the daddy, the police officer. Sometimes it is not apparent—your child may imitate your manner and behavior and become more

and more like you without either of you being aware of it. But the drive to imitate the ways of adults is always active, a powerful learning asset and a responsibility for the adults who are the models.

* *Concerned with the here and now.* Kindergarten children know about yesterday and tomorrow, but their life is lived today. They want to experience everything in their home, their classroom, their school yard. For them, what they do in school is neither about the past nor about the future. It is about their personal world, just as it is right now.

Good kindergarten teachers provide for these qualities in children. They create opportunities for children to pursue their curiosity, to use all of their senses in their exploration, to expand their minds. They arrange for abundant hands-on physical activity, for movement, for frequent changes of pace. They are respectful of the emotional bond they have with their children and aware that they serve as models of adult behavior. And they create a classroom environment, a here and now, that is rich in its intellectual and social opportunities for learning.

WHEN SHOULD YOUR CHILD ENTER SCHOOL

The legal age for entering kindergarten varies from state to state. Most children enter kindergarten from about age four and a half to about age five and a half. Chronologically alone, the variation is one of almost 20 percent! When differences in individual rates and patterns of development are added, one understands the need to adjust to each child's particular nature. Parents and teachers should not expect all kindergarten children to be at the same level of maturity or to profit equally from the same activities.

What is important is that each child experience success on his own terms. Whatever "catching up" with others is necessary will happen later.

There is a standing debate about whether children—especially boys, who generally mature more slowly—should begin kindergarten while still four years of age or in the early months of five. Those who argue for later entry say that younger children are not ready for formal schooling. They say such children will experience difficulty and perhaps failure, which will plague them ever after.

Whatever the merits of this position may be, the authors believe that as a practical matter the argument is irrelevant. In today's world, most children will enter kindergarten when they are of legal age to do so. Therefore, the job of the school and of the kindergarten teacher is to follow a program that is appropriate to each child's individual level of development. Given our current state of knowledge about how children learn and grow, there is simply no reason why this cannot be done.

THE JOB OF TEACHER, PARENT, AND CHILD

Kindergarten children are learners by nature. Thus, everyone's job is simple. The job of the teacher is to create an environment that nurtures children's natural instinct to learn. The job of the parent is to support the work of the teacher and the child with confidence in the child's powers. And the job of the child, with a little help from his friends, is simply to be himself.

Readiness for the Kindergarten

Most children do well in kindergarten. No special preparation is or should be required. In general, the parents' responsibility is to boost their child's confidence and to prepare him to enjoy this exciting new experience. The last thing a beginning kindergarten child needs is an anxious parent worried about the child's "success" in school.

However, there are certain skills and knowledge you can help your child acquire in advance that will ease the transition from home to school and that will make your child's school experience more rewarding.

In this regard, it is important to remember that the goals of the kindergarten are both academic and social. During the kindergarten year, children will begin to learn to read and write, to do simple arithmetic, to acquire rudimentary study skills and work habits. They will also learn to be responsible members of a group—to share materials, to take turns, to be quiet when appropriate, to take care of their own belongings, to cooperate with others in accomplishing a task. All of these skills will be needed as children continue their schooling. Thus, in helping your child get ready for kindergarten you should think about social behavior as well as academic readiness.

READINESS CHECKLIST

Required Skills

By the time they enter kindergarten, all children should be able to do the following:

- Tell their name, address, and telephone number.
- Tell their parents' names.
- Know the way to get to school and the way to get home.
- Travel alone in the immediate neighborhood—to the store, to the playground, to a friend's.
- Accomplish simple jobs at home—shutting the door, getting a cup, putting toys away.
- Care for themselves at toilet without help.
- Wash their own face and hands.
- Take their boots off and put them on by themselves (parents can help by buying boots that are simple to put on and fasten).
- Take their sweater or jacket off and put it back on, even if it's inside out.
- Use buttons or zippers without help (again, parents can help by buying simple clothing).
- Play reasonably well with other children of the same age—without excessive crying, fighting, or teasing.
- Make their wants known in short, easy sentences (as opposed to pointing or crying).
- Listen quietly while being read a short story or a poem.

Children acquire most of these skills through normal family living. However, if your family life is irregular, you may wish to spend more time with your child in the months before kindergarten begins. Remember, the more attention you give your child, and the more you expect of him during the preschool years, the better the school years ahead will be.

Optional Skills

If your child can do all of the things listed above, he is ready for kindergarten. However, there are other skills that will enhance your child's school experience. Ideally, children entering kindergarten should be able to do the following:

- Recognize their own printed name.
- Tell their right from their left.
- Tie their own shoes.
- Use crayons and chalk.
- Fill in outlined figures reasonably well (without excessive scribbling).
- Cut with blunt scissors.
- Match simple colors.
- Recognize basic colors: red, orange, yellow, blue, green, brown, black.
- Describe simple dimensions: big or little, tall or short, fat or thin.
- Describe simple quantities: one or two, a few or a lot, some or all.
- Identify simple shapes: circles, squares, triangles.
- Draw or copy a square.
- Fit blocks and toys together.
- Understand and use simple spatial concepts: up, down, in, out, behind, under.

If your prekindergarten child can do these things, rejoice! If not, don't panic. Kindergarten is a place to learn, not to conduct postgraduate research.

Parents can help children acquire such abilities by talking with them, reading to them, listening to them, asking questions and discussing the answers. In general, the more communication, the better. Be patient with your child's questions. Learn to ask questions and play games that reward knowledge ("I'm thinking of something in this room that's *red*") or provoke thought ("What do you suppose would happen if . . ."). Encourage your child to paint and draw, to look at books and magazines, to listen to music. Let the child try to "fix" things, to "cook," to clean up. Play games together. Take trips. Have fun. The years go by too quickly, and what your child may miss, you will miss also.

PRESCHOOL

What about preschool programs for three- or four-year-olds? Today, about one third of the nation's children of that age are enrolled in some preschool program. Do such programs increase a child's chances for success in kindergarten and the later years of schooling?

The evidence suggests that preschool programs are not necessary for success in school. After all, two of every three children do *not* participate in such programs, and most of them are successful. However, recent studies show that preschool does make a positive difference for many children.

Early studies of the effects of preschool, conducted mostly on children of poverty in the late 1960s, suggested that children's test scores increased when they were enrolled in some program—but only temporarily. Unless the regular school continued to devote special attention to such children, the test-score advantage disappeared within a few short years.

More recent studies, conducted in the 1980s, have been better able to determine the long-range effects of preschool. These studies show that children who have attended preschool tend to repeat fewer grades and to be assigned to remedial classes less often. They suggest that preschool attendance influences children's attitudes and behavior in ways that make them more successful later on. Children who have learned how to cooperate in a group, to concentrate on their own work, to listen to the teacher, tend to do better in school and to progress more satisfactorily. And these findings seem to apply as much to middle-class children as to those from poorer families.

All in all, this seems to be welcome news for all parents. If you have to work, you can send your child to a well-run preschool program without guilt. If you or your spouse stays at home but *choose* to enroll your child in a preschool program, you can do so with the knowledge that you may be giving your child an advantage. And if you choose to keep your child at home until kindergarten, you have the successful experience of millions of others to support your decision—plus the fun of being with your child.

The rest of your child's life and schooling should be so easy.

REGISTRATION AND SCREENING

In most schools, you will be asked to register your child before the school year actually begins—a few days before school opens, or even as early as the preceding spring. Typically, you will be asked to come to the school with your child to fill out forms and to provide certain information. You will meet with a secretary and perhaps with a nurse, a psychologist, your child's future teacher, or the school principal.

In most cases, this will be your child's first contact with the school. Be aware of its huge importance to him! What may seem to you to be a perfunctory bureaucratic procedure is, for your child, the first formal step into the official world away from home. It is important that you make the occasion pleasant so that your child forms a good impression of the school. It also provides an opportunity for you to make your own acquaintance with school personnel.

Walk or ride to school with your child and point out landmarks along the way. Show him the door to enter in the morning and, if he is bused, the place to wait for the bus in the afternoon. If possible, take him to the classroom and point out the block corner, the doll corner, the easels, the piano. Talk openly about your child with school personnel, and if you are able to do so, volunteer to help out when needed.

In many schools the formal registration procedure will be limited to collecting basic information: your child's name, address, date of birth, immunization record, emergency telephone numbers. In some schools, however, screening procedures have become quite elaborate. New York State, for example, requires that local school districts develop procedures for identifying children who may be gifted or talented or who may have handicapping conditions. In one community, the procedures include the following:

Screening Device	*Done By*
Physical and developmental history	School nurse
Vision and hearing test	School nurse
Motor, language, and cognitive development tests	School psychologist
Emotional and social history	School psychologist
Articulation (speech) and language tests	Speech teacher
Observation of child in group setting	Kindergarten teacher
Intellectual, creativity, artistic, and leadership questionnaire	Kindergarten teacher

Whatever procedures are required for your child, treat them as significant and positive. Be excited and happy that your child is about to take this big new step.

UN-READINESS

Suppose you feel that your child is *not* ready to begin kindergarten. How can you be sure? What signs should you watch for, and what should you do?

As we have said, most children will begin attending school when they are of legal age to do so. However, in many states children are not *required* to attend school until they are six years old. Parents have the right not to enroll their children in school until then. In many situations, you can decide whether your child should begin kindergarten one year or the next.

In the authors' experience, the number of children who should not begin school with their agemates is relatively small. However, individual rates of growth do vary. For reasons that we do not yet fully understand, some children develop more slowly than others. Some children who are very bright, who may even be able to read a bit, are not socially or physically ready to attend school. They may not be ready to cooperate with other children, or they may not yet be physically coordinated enough to manage scissors and crayons or be able to sit still in one place.

If your child has not yet mastered the skills in the "Required Skills" part of the "Readiness Checklist" above, or if he is extremely reluctant to go to school—to the point of clinging and crying, even after the first few days—you may wish to consider deferring kindergarten for a year. Remember that some experts believe that many children begin school too early. By waiting until your child develops more fully, you give him a better chance to experience immediate success when school does begin.

For the same reasons, parents should think twice before seeking early admission to kindergarten for their child. If your school system requires children to be five years old on or before January 1 and your child's fifth birthday is on January 6, you may be tempted to try to persuade the authorities to permit your child to enter with those only a few days older. But remember the importance to your child's entire school experience of a solid, successful beginning. He may be much better off for waiting.

Your esteem as a parent should depend on how well you know your child and how wisely you guide his development. It should not depend upon whether your child begins kindergarten at four and a half or five and a half. Few children, if any, have led happier or more successful lives because they began kindergarten a few months earlier. Some may have been hurt because they were forced to begin school before they were ready to do so. In the long span of your child's future life, a few more months of quiet growth and getting ready may be a small but valuable investment.

Getting Started: The First Days

Now it is about to begin. You have decided that your child will start kindergarten, registration has been completed, you've laid out the school clothes. Perhaps your child has attended a preschool program and has become accustomed to being separated from parents and to playing and working with other children and adults. Or perhaps this will be your child's first real separation from the home. Either way, the step is momentous. The relatively casual, intimate environment of home or preschool is giving way to one that many children see as large, formal, and threatening—and one that will claim most of their waking hours for one day out of two for the next thirteen years of their lives.

Most of this book is about what children and teachers do in classrooms. But parents should not minimize the effect of the total school setting on children's feelings and behavior, nor should they underestimate the way in which school-life problems outside the classroom can impede learning. The child who is afraid of the bully on the bus or who worries because he does not know how to tell the teacher when he has to go to the bathroom does not have a clear mind ready for poetry or computer science.

Here are some ways in which parents can help children have a good experience during the first few days of school.

BREAKFAST

Get yourself and your child up early enough to eat a calm, unhurried breakfast. Don't begin the day in an atmosphere of tension by not allowing proper time to wash, dress, eat, chat, and say good-bye. If necessary, adjust your child's sleep schedule a few weeks before school begins so that he will be awake and alert when the time arrives. And keep things as normal as possible. If your child usually eats cornflakes, give him cornflakes. If you feel compelled to get out the oatmeal, eat it yourself.

WHAT TO WEAR

Dressing up for school is largely out of fashion. Wearing clean, comfortable play clothes to school lets your child sit on the floor, paint, and take part in other activities without worrying about "good clothes." Be sure that whatever your child wears is large enough and simple enough to take off and put on alone. You may wish to visit the school during the preceding spring or talk to other parents to see what children are wearing. (This may be particularly important if you have just moved to a new community.) You don't want your child to be uncomfortable because the other children regard him as odd.

WHAT TO BRING

Most schools will tell you, either beforehand or during the first few days, what children are required to bring with them to school. Some schools, for example, may ask children to bring a pair of sneakers for gym, an old "paint" shirt, money for milk or snacks. We suggest that you wait to see what your child's school requires. Sending the child off with a batch of sharpened pencils and a loose-leaf notebook may just create problems.

SAYING GOOD-BYE

Wherever you say good-bye to your child on the first few mornings—at home, at the bus stop, at the school yard—make it quick, light, and reassuring. A warm hug and a kiss and a promise that you (or grandma or brother or the baby-sitter) will be waiting at home or ready to pick them up at school at the stated hour is all that is required. Don't communicate to your child whatever anxiety or separation pangs you may feel. We have actually known children who felt guilty because their leaving made their parents feel so sad.

Many parents feel a temporary sense of loss when their children go off to school. You may want to plan to visit a friend or engage in some other social activity during the first day or two. It's all right to tell your child that you will miss him, but try to emphasize how proud you are of him and how happy. Over the long span of years ahead, part of your job as parent is gradually to let go. Here is an important occasion on which to begin.

THE WALK TO SCHOOL

If your child is to walk to school, he should know the way before the first day arrives. Perhaps you have already walked the route together a few times, chatting about the landmarks along the way. However, if you are able to do so, you still may wish to accompany your child on the first few days. (Ask him how he feels about it—your presence may be embarrassing.) If an older sibling attends the same school, ask him to accompany your kindergarten child. Older children (of elementary-school age at least) enjoy the feeling of responsibility, and the presence of an older brother or sister can make a child feel more secure, especially at first. Sometimes there are bothersome dogs or difficult traffic crossings to contend with. Don't minimize these problems; show your child exactly what to do. And be assertive. Introduce yourselves to the policeman or the school-crossing guard. If necessary, speak to the owner of the dog. We love animals, but your child has a right to walk to school without being terrorized.

THE BUS RIDE

Many children must take a bus to get to school. For some, the ride will be a short, pleasant trip across town. For others, the journey may last as long as an hour, during which time adult supervision will be minimal.

The majority of school principals will attest that most behavior problems among children are apt to occur on buses, during lunch, and in bathrooms. It is at those times and in those settings that children's behavior is least structured and supervised and that the "ruler of the school yard" holds sway. Buses are a particular problem, because they may not be under the direct control of school authorities and because there is normally only one driver to manage the bus and to deal with up to sixty or more children of varied ages and dispositions.

You can help your child cope with this potentially unpleasant situation. First of all, make sure your child knows which bus to take, both going to school and coming home. Show him where to wait for it and what signs to look for on it. (Children of kindergarten age are often very literal. If the bus is called the "red" bus or the "blue" bus but is painted yellow, explain this contradiction.) Introduce your child to the driver. Most school drivers come to know and like the children they transport. If there is an older sibling or an older child from the neighborhood, enlist his support. And do not hesitate to talk to school authorities if problems do arise. (Some communities have solved discipline problems on buses by assigning paid aides or parent volunteers as chaperones.)

CAR POOLS

Perhaps you live in an area where your child will go to school by car pool. Parents may take turns driving a small number of children to school each day. If so, you should know the names, addresses, and telephone numbers of all the participating parents, and you should be familiar with the cars they drive. Your child should be able to recognize each parent driver (you don't want your child to accept a ride from a stranger) and know the names of the other children. Your child should also know where and when to be picked up and what to do if the car does not arrive. (Getting signals straight is particularly important if you participate in a rainy-day car pool, that is, one that operates only in inclement weather.) You should establish safe-driving rules for all participating children: wear seat belts, lock the door, get out on the sidewalk side, wait to cross the street. Car pools can be fun for children and even for adults, but they are serious business, worthy of a few precautions.

MEETING THE TEACHER

In most cases, you and your child will have met the teacher some time before the first day of school. Even so, if you are able to, you may wish to introduce yourself and your child again on the first day. (Remember, you have only one teacher to remember, but the teacher must get to know up to thirty or more children and their parents.) If you do not accompany your child to school, be sure that he can say the teacher's name. Tell him to mind the teacher. Speak about the teacher as someone who has your confidence and respect.

LUNCH

Many kindergarten children attend half-day sessions and are not in school at lunchtime. For the growing number who attend full-day kindergarten, lunch is an important time.

During the lunch period, your child will have more freedom of activity than during most of the rest of the school day. It is a time for being with friends, relaxing, letting off steam. It is also a time when problems can arise—of loneliness or uncertainty, of children being rude or unkind to one another. During the first few days of school, ask your child what he did at lunchtime, and be alert for any problems that may be suggested. And again, do not hesitate to talk to the teacher or other school personnel if you feel the need to do so.

As for lunch itself, schools vary widely in their practices. Some have cafeterias and sell hot lunches. Some serve only sandwiches and milk. Some provide a free lunch daily. In some schools, children must bring their lunch from home and eat it at their desk or at some other designated location. If so, the school nurse or the PTA may suggest guidelines for nutritious lunches. Learn how your child's school manages lunch, and tell your child exactly what to expect.

THE BATHROOM

Kindergarten children's initial anxieties about toileting should not be overestimated. We know of children who have soiled their pants because they did not know how to find the bathroom or because they did not know what words to use to tell the teacher that they had to go. Most teachers will speedily establish satisfactory procedures for children to follow. However, you can help by making sure your child knows how to make his needs known and is not afraid to do so and by telling the teacher in advance about any special problem he may have.

STAYING IN TOUCH

In the authors' experience, children who go off to kindergarten are of four categories:

1. Those who leave easily and adjust readily.
2. Those who are reluctant to leave—who cling to their parents and who may even have an upset stomach on the first day or two—but then make a happy adjustment after the first few days.
3. Those who leave reluctantly and fail to adjust after several days or weeks.
4. Those who leave easily, even eagerly, but begin to develop re-

sistance once the reality and permanence of the school situation sink in.

Of the four categories, children in the latter two bear the most watching. Such children may develop headaches or say that they feel ill. They may talk about how a teacher or another child treats them badly. In such cases, it is important to get to the root of the problem as soon as possible. Most children can adjust to school with continuing help from a sensitive teacher and parents. Some few may be demonstrating that they are not yet ready for school.

For these reasons, it is important to stay in close touch with your child's feelings during the first days of school.

Ask your child each afternoon or evening how his day was. What did he make? What games did he play? Was so-and-so on the bus? How did he behave? What did they have for snack? Give your child every opportunity to tell you what he feels good about and what worries him. Listen to what is said, and listen "between the lines."

Throughout, maintain a positive and cheerful tone. Your child is taking giant steps in his development. Be excited! Be proud!

The Idea of
Kindergarten

The kindergarten, German for "children's garden," dates to the early nineteenth century. Friedrich Froebel, a German teacher and writer, believed that young children's native abilities would unfold naturally in an atmosphere of guided play, self-directed activity, and learning by doing. His program took its shape from the nature of the child: it was, as we would say today, child-centered rather than adult-centered or content-centered. The idea took hold in many countries, but nowhere so pervasively as in the United States.

For many years in the United States most children's first school experience was in the kindergarten. The program provided a comfortable transition between the home and the school and promoted readiness for the first grade. The emphasis was upon social adjustment, not upon academic skills. Kindergarten was play time; serious learning began in grade one.

However, today's kindergarten children are different. Almost one third of all American children have been enrolled in some kind of preschool program. Society is more mobile, and many parents and children have been exposed to different experiences through travel. Many children live with a single parent or in some other nontraditional family setting. And, most of all, today's kindergarten children have grown up watching television.

Statistics show that by the time a five-year-old child enters kindergarten, he may have spent up to 5,000 hours watching television. The effect of this experience on children's knowledge, thought processes, and relationship to the adult world can scarcely be overemphasized.

Because of their exposure to television, children come to school knowing more than children of earlier generations. Through programs like *Sesame Street* and *Electric Company*, they have been exposed to reading readiness activities traditionally associated with formal schooling. Through comedies and game shows and commercials, and even the news, they have been exposed to the adult values of society, to what is sold, to how it's sold, to what is made to seem valuable. They have watched how other people live or are made to seem to live. And they know that they are part of a larger world not bounded by the experience and values of their family, their neighborhood, their school.

Television watching has an impact of its own, separate from the content of its programs. Many children have developed mental habits appropriate to a "television culture" rather than a "book culture." In order to read, a child must master the skills of written language. But to watch television, no skill is required and no gratification must be postponed.

When the set is turned on, there is instant reward. The images are quick and fleeting; they communicate through immediate sensory impact, not through sequential thought and imagination. If the program is dull, a quick turn of the dial produces another. (Many experienced kindergarten teachers talk about their increasing difficulty in getting today's kindergarten children to focus their attention on a game or task for any length of time.

Furthermore, the world of commercial television is open to all viewers, adults and children alike. No longer can parents and the school limit the child's knowledge to what seems appropriate by carefully selecting the books and films to which the child is exposed. Violence, greed, and folly are not confined to a few "bad" programs that the child should not be allowed to watch—

they are everywhere. On the surface, at least, the innocence of childhood is becoming a thing of the past.

As a result of these and other changes, American kindergartens have come to vary widely in both form and content. For many years, most kindergarten classes met for half a day only, either during the morning or the afternoon. (In some situations, the full class would meet each morning and a small number of children would stay or return in the afternoon.) Today, more and more kindergartens meet for the full school day. The change reflects the belief that more time is required to prepare children academically and the need of working parents for full-day child care. If your school system offers a half-day program, you may want to ask what plans it may have for full-day attendance.

The content of kindergarten programs varies. Some schools continue to emphasize the traditional skills of social readiness. Others have full-fledged programs in reading and writing. In general, there is a growing tendency to increase the emphasis on developing readiness skills in language, reading, writing, and mathematics.

Some experts believe that this new emphasis puts too much pressure on children. They believe that children need more time to grow and develop, that it is better for the child to wait another year than to be harmed through early failure. Other experts claim that many children of kindergarten age have learned to read and write successfully and that failure to challenge the child's mind will stunt his mental growth.

In the authors' view, both sides are right, as is so often true in controversies. Children vary in age, abilities, experience, and rates of maturation. Some are not yet ready to read and should not be pushed to do so. Some are already reading or are obviously ready to learn, and they should be encouraged and helped. The good kindergarten teacher will provide a stimulating mental climate for your child at his individual stage of development—without pressure, restraint, or stigma for any child.

In general, the goals of the kindergarten program are

- To help children acquire social readiness skills for cooperating with other children and adults in a group setting.
- To help children acquire academic readiness skills for speaking, listening, reading, writing, and mathematics.
- To expand children's knowledge of their environment and to stimulate their curiosity, imagination, and powers of observation and reasoning.

How do kindergarten teachers organize time and activity to meet these goals?

The Kindergarten Day

The kindergarten room reflects the nature of the kindergarten program. Enter any reasonably well-equipped kindergarten classroom and you are apt to see

- A large open area where the whole class can sit together on the floor.
- Small movable tables and chairs.
- A number of activity centers or corners with equipment for housekeeping, playing with blocks, painting, woodworking, writing, doing mathematics.
- Bulletin boards or charts for keeping track of the days, attendance, who is doing what.
- Stacks of books, arranged so that children have easy access.
- Cubbies or lockers in which children store their belongings.

If the class is lucky, there may also be

- A sink for painting, science experiments, and cleaning up.
- A piano.
- A phonograph with headsets.
- A computer screen and keyboard.
- Animals in cages: mice, gerbils, chickens.

Throughout the day, children move from large group to small group and from one activity center to another, partly at their own choice and partly according to rules and schedules determined by the teacher. A child's day in a well-run kindergarten is a balance of activities, including

- Time for play and time for work.
- Time for working with three or four other children and time for meeting with the whole class.
- Time for being alone with the teacher and time for being with the group.
- Time for physical exercise and time for being quiet.
- Time for the creative arts and time for academic areas.

Good kindergarten teachers plan the day carefully, paying close attention to the transitions between activities—they know that children often respond as much to how things are done as to what is done. One group of experienced kindergarten teachers developed the following model of a kindergarten day, being careful to point out that the model would vary with the teacher, the class, the time of year, and other factors:

9:00–9:30	*Meeting Time for Whole Class*
	Opening activities: announcements, the weather, birthdays
	Planning for the day
	Show and tell
9:30–10:30	*Work Period*
	Work at learning centers: art corner, library, writing table, housekeeping center, block corner, science area, game and building corner, listening area, computer center, dramatic play

10:30–10:50	*Quiet Time*
	Snack, discussion, singing
10:50–11:10	*Recess*
	Outdoors when possible
11:10–12:00	*Direct-Instruction Activity*
	Writing, science, class projects, etc. Preparation for lunch
12:00–1:00	*Lunch and Play*
1:00–1:20	*Quiet Time and Rest*
1:20–2:00	*Art or Music*
2:00–2:30	*Active Play*
	Indoor or out
2:30–3:00	*Closing Time*
	Story time, summary of day, preparation for dismissal

Such a model, however useful, does not convey the richness of activity that characterizes most kindergarten classrooms. Consider the scene described below.

A Tuesday morning in early December. The Thanksgiving decorations still fill the room. The children are at the learning centers; the teacher calls it play time. On the wall hangs a large perforated board with S-hooks on which the children have hung name cards, to show which center they will be in. In the kitchen corner, three girls and a boy are a "family," doing chores and cooking dinner. Another group is at a long table, measuring rice in cups of different sizes. Two girls play a game of Concentration, using picture cards. A boy licks stickers of baseball players and pastes them in a book—a Keith Hernandez, a Pete Rose. Several children are at easels, painting large, colorful houses with tempera. In the block corner, three children cooperate in building a tower; three others take some of the blocks and play alone. Children move freely about the room. The teacher is getting cookies ready for snack time, a small boy hugging her leg.

An observer notes these features:

- The children are enjoying themselves. Meanwhile, however, they *are* learning. The children with the rice are observing, estimating, measuring, watching what happens to the same mass in different-size containers. The three children in the block corner are learning to work as a group.
- The children play together or work at the same task even though they are at very different levels of ability.
- There is much imaginative play, as in the kitchen corner, and much use of the imagination in other activity, as in the painting.
- By this time of year, the children know the rules. They go to the centers readily, find the right materials, and play within the permitted levels of noise and movement. They are learning to be constructive members of a social group.

Language Development in the Kindergarten

Speech has often been called our most distinctly human activity. Our closest animal cousins, the chimpanzees and gorillas, can, by the time they are a few months old, outrun, outclimb, and outmuscle human babies of the same age. What makes our children (and most of their parents) unique is their power to acquire and use language. By the use of language, in all its forms, human beings can communicate with one another about themselves and their environment, can develop categories of thought to perceive and reflect about experience, can think about their world in order to control and to change it.

To a large extent, the work of the schools throughout the grades is to nurture the development of this miraculous capacity for language. Certainly, children's success in school largely depends upon their success in learning to speak, listen, read, and write.

Three ideas about language underlie the language programs of most American schools.

1. *Language is a symbol for experience.* Human beings have developed a complex system of spoken and written symbols to stand for the things, actions, and relationships in their environment. At the most primitive level, these sounds and letters are closely re-

lated to what can be immediately perceived by the senses: the car is moving, the glass is full, I am hungry. At a more sophisticated level, the symbols stand for categories and relationships that cannot be immediately perceived but that can be inferred from past and present experience: automobile production, dairy farming, world famine relief. The language of kindergarten children is still closely tied to direct experience. Parents and teachers help children to increase their vocabulary and language power by associating new words with specific things or actions: the stove is *hot*, the book is *under* the table, the round one is a *circle*. At this age, unless the child has had the specific experience of feeling the heat of the stove, of finding the book under the table, of seeing or touching the circle, the words themselves mean little or nothing. (How often we hear children of this age using or misusing words whose meaning they do not know, swear words, for example.) Therefore, much of the language curriculum of the schools involves associating new words and phrases, in speech and in writing, with the experiences children have in class or out.

2. *The purpose of language is communication.* This idea is self-evident to most children but seems to have been forgotten by some schools. Children are born with a drive to acquire and use speech. From infancy on, their initially random sounds become more and more closely adapted to the language environment around them (usually the language of the family) precisely because they wish to communicate with others. By the time they reach kindergarten age, this ability to use speech to communicate is usually fairly well developed. There are important language skills still to be learned. In good schools, however, these skills are taught not in isolation, but as a by-product of children's desire to communicate with other people: their teacher, their classmates, their parents, or others of importance to them.

3. *Language is a continuum of listening, speaking, reading, and writing.* All forms of language are related. The child hears the word and imitates its sound until he gets it "right." (Once he associates it with a specific thing, quality, or action, he knows the word and

can use it to communicate with others.) Now he can listen and speak. Later, he can recognize the symbols people use to denote individual spoken words—he sees that "reading is talk written down." Now he has begun to read. At about the same time, he learns to make his own symbols through drawings or signs (as the cavemen depicted their experience through the drawings on the cave walls) and, eventually, to use the same symbols that others use (the letters and words of our language). Now he has begun to write. For most children, with normal neurological capacity and typical life experience, the constant shifting from listening to speaking to reading to writing and back comes easily and naturally. Good kindergarten language teachers understand this functional relationship and build upon children's oral speech abilities to develop readiness skills in reading and writing.

Between infancy and kindergarten age, the language growth of children is phenomenal. During these years, children make connections between sounds and experience, internalize the grammatical patterns of their language, and acquire a sizable speaking vocabulary. (Estimates are that children of kindergarten age have speaking vocabularies of from about 2,500 to over 12,000 words.) Whether or not they have attended preschool programs, most children enter kindergarten with a solid base of spoken language upon which teachers can build.

However, just as kindergarten children vary in age, physical growth, ability to get along in a group, mental development, and life experience, so they vary in language development as well. The good kindergarten program tries to meet these differences. Children from home settings where the use of language is limited need more experience and time to develop language concepts and a larger speaking vocabulary before attempting more formal reading readiness activities. (Headstart and similar preschool programs have demonstrated success with such children.) Children from home settings in which language use is prized—where they are encouraged to talk and to ask questions, where they are often read to—need opportunities to expand upon this richness. They should not be limited to the meager resources provided by some formal reading readiness programs.

In general, the job of the kindergarten language program is to build upon the capacity that children bring to school in order to develop the reading and writing readiness skills needed for success in first grade.

What are these skills, and how does the kindergarten go about developing them?

READING/WRITING READINESS SKILLS

Research and practice have shown that certain "readiness" skills are necessary for children to succeed in learning to read and write. If necessary, these skills are taught in first grade. However, the child who masters them by the end of kindergarten is more likely to begin reading quickly once first grade begins and to be a confident and happy learner.

Schools and experts vary in their description of these skills. However, in general, five categories can be identified: auditory discrimination, visual discrimination, sound-symbol correspondence, perceptual-motor, and oral language skills.

Auditory Discrimination Skills

Children must learn to recognize common sounds in their environment and to distinguish between them. They must come to understand the concepts of volume, pitch, direction, duration, sequence, accent, tempo, repetition, and contrast. Eventually, they must come to distinguish the sounds of the letters in our alphabet—in the kindergarten, especially the sounds made by the initial consonants in words. (The child must be able to distinguish the *sound* of the letter *d* from the *sound* of *t*, the *sound* of *m* from the *sound* of *n*.)

Visual Discrimination Skills

Children must learn to recognize common objects and experiences through depiction of them in photographs, painting, and pantomime. They must learn to identify basic colors and geometric shapes and be able to match objects by color, shape, or size. They must be able to distinguish left from right and up from down, and to follow a progression from left to right and up to down. They must be able to tell a figure from the background, to notice details in a picture, and to discern simple visual patterns. Eventually, they must be able to recognize and name uppercase and lowercase letters. (The child must be able to distinguish the *sight* of *d* from the *sight* of *t*, the *sight* of *m* from the *sight* of *n*.)

Sound-Symbol Correspondence Skills

Eventually, the child must be able to associate uppercase and lowercase letters with their names and with the sounds they represent. He must know that *d* is called *dee* and stands for the sound at the beginning of the word *dog*. Most children will make good initial progress at these skills during kindergarten. Few will master all of the sound-symbol skills until later in the grades.

Perceptual-Motor Skills

Children must mature sufficiently to be able to use the small muscles of their hands and fingers and to coordinate the movements with what they see. They must refine these skills so that they can assemble simple puzzles, finger-paint pictures, mold clay, string beads, pour liquids, use scissors. They must learn to hold crayons, Magic Markers and pencils, to color simple pictures within the lines, to trace lines and shapes in the air and on paper, to copy lines and shapes without tracing. Eventually, they must be able to copy letters and words, to print their name, to write the letter that matches the sound.

Oral Language Skills

As we have said, children come to kindergarten with substantial skill in speaking and listening. However, during the kindergarten year, these skills must be further developed and refined. Children must learn to listen, to remember, to follow directions, to note details, to understand the main idea. They must use and expand upon their speaking vocabularies to explain ideas, to describe objects and events, to express their own feelings or those of real or imaginary people. They should come to enjoy the sharing of experience through language and take pleasure in learning and using new words.

Successful progress in mastering these five categories of reading/writing readiness skills all but assures success in learning to read and write.

TEACHING READING/WRITING READINESS SKILLS

How do kindergarten teachers help children learn these skills? In a well-run kindergarten, most of the activity and even the physical environment itself contribute to the development of reading/writing readiness skills. From the time the children arrive in the morning and discuss the day's schedule, the weather, and any unusual local or national events to the time they leave, when they summarize the day's happenings and say their good-byes, they are involved in sights and sounds and activities that encourage and reinforce the use of language.

Around the room, on bulletin boards, blackboards, easels, desk tops, hanging from string or wire, pasted or propped beneath objects, are charts, pictures, posters, paintings, signs that reflect the developing language program. Early in the year, these are colors, rainbows, circles, squares, triangles. Later pictures are added recalling the experiences children have had—the rainstorm, the eggs hatching, the trip to the zoo—and the names of the children who made the pictures. Later, too, there are increasingly more labels for the names of things—the desk, the sink, the clock, the crayons—all placed so that children begin to associate the sight of the word with the thing itself. Books themselves—bright, inviting picture books, some with words, some without—are abundant and readily accessible to the children. Everywhere the child sees physical reinforcement of language use and language growth.

The activity in the room is also language-oriented. As a total class and in small groups in the activity corner, children engage in action and then use language to describe what they have done. Whether they are painting pictures, making cookies, building kites, caring for plants, feeding animals, or working with the computer, all activity becomes a subject for talk, for thinking about and sharing one's experience. Children have opportunities to be the speaker and to listen and react. Later, they can make pictures or even "write" about their experiences.

The role of the teacher in this activity is crucial. Not only does she plan and equip the room and all its activity centers, she constantly interacts with the children and helps them interact with one another. Whatever the activity, she helps out, encourages, and looks for opportunities to expand thinking and develop skills. Good teachers know the children and have the knack of asking the productive question at the right time. Open-ended questions, which encourage children to think ("What do you suppose would happen if we made this one smaller?"), are better than closed-ended questions, which require little response or simply give the teacher the right answer ("What's the name of the small one?"). All kindergarten teachers seek to stimulate children's language use and development in these ways; some are more skillful in doing so than others.

The following scene is typical:

A winter Monday morning. The children have hung up their coats, put their lunches in their cubbies, and are seated on the floor around the teacher.

"Who knows where we go first thing this morning?" asks the teacher.

A child waves his hand, barely able to contain himself. "Library," he announces proudly.

"Absolutely right," says the teacher. "I hope you all remembered to bring your books?" One child asks if he may keep his book another week. "You may renew it," says the teacher. "Does anyone know what *renew* means?"

One child says, "Keep it longer."

"That's right," says the teacher. "That's what it means in this case. If you like your book so much that you would like to keep it another week we ask the librarian if we may *renew* our book. That means 'take it out again.' "

"Now, it's time for show and tell," continues the teacher. "Who would like to be first?"

A child runs to the door to the outside, opens it, and brings a paper cup to the front of the group. She stays physically so close to the teacher that she is almost on her lap. The child says, "I have snow in a special cup to see how long I can keep it."

"What do you think will happen to the snow in the cup when you bring it inside?" asks the teacher.

The child says, "It will melt."

"What does *melt* mean?" asks the teacher.

"Turn to water," says a little girl with braids.

"What would happen is we put a glass of water outside today?" continues the teacher.

"It would freeze," replies the little girl with the cup.

"What does *freeze* mean?" asks the teacher.

"Turn to ice," answers a boy in back.

A brief conversation ensues about cold, temperatures, and so on. The children are fascinated and not at all aware that they have had a vocabulary lesson.

At other times, the teaching of language skills is more direct. Almost all kindergarten teachers read stories and poems aloud, play word games, involve children in puppetry or dramatic play. Some teach formal language lessons, either to the whole class or to small groups of children. Early in the year, such lessons might be about colors or shapes or left-to-right progression. For example, in a lesson about circles, the teacher gathers the class and shows them a large box containing a variety of round objects: coins, paper plates, bottle tops, coasters. She asks the children to remove the objects one at a time and to identify each for the group. She asks them to describe how it looks and how it feels. She has the children trace the shape of each object. She displays all the objects where everyone can see, arranging them from left to right. She asks what the objects have in common. From the discussion, she elicits (or supplies, if necessary) the words *round* and *circle*. She has children look in the room for other objects that are round. She has children draw, cut, and paste circles—big and small, of varied colors—and make circle designs. If the room has a computer, she may have the children attempt to create circles on the screen. She asks the children to summarize what they have done. She has the children hang round objects about the room, and labels them "round." Later, she reinforces the lesson by having children bring in round objects from home and by having them match circular shapes and distinguish them from other shapes.

Later in the year, such language lessons might be about specific letters—the name of the letter and the sound it represents. For example, in a lesson about the sound of the initial consonant *m*, the teacher gathers a group of the children (some or all of the class) and shows them a doll of a monkey and a box full of objects beginning with the letter *m*, such as masks, mittens, marbles, milk, mustard, and Magic Markers. She says that the monkey has brought the box so they can play a game—they are to look at the objects and see if they can find something that is the same about all of them. Children take turns removing objects from the box and naming them. If a child has trouble, other children or the teacher helps. As they proceed, the teacher asks the children to summarize thus far by repeating the names of the objects already identified. Once all the objects have been named, the teacher asks the children what they have in common. If necessary, she supplies the answer—they all begin with the sound m-m-m. The children make the sound. She asks if they can guess why the monkey brought the box. She has the children find other objects in the room whose names begin with the sound m-m-m. Later, she introduces the written symbol for the sound (the letter *m*) and provides many opportunities for children to find the letter, to make its sound, and to copy or draw its shape.

Formal lessons of this kind are fairly common in American kindergartens. In very good classrooms, teachers also develop reading/writing readiness skills by helping children build upon their use of oral language. At first in a group, and later individually, children "dictate" their account of an experience to the teacher. They may tell about people or events at home or in the neighborhood, about places they have been, about current or seasonal events, about things that have happened in the classroom, about dreams or wishes—about everything, in short, that has personal meaning for them. The teacher writes or prints their "stories" for them, and the children then "read" their story back to the teacher and to others in the class. They see immediately that writing is speech written down and that reading and writing go hand in hand. They begin to develop a *sight vocabulary*—words that they recognize and understand in print—because the words they see are their own. And they have the full range of their speaking vocabularies to draw upon, a much richer resource than the vocabulary banks of most formal reading readiness programs. By the end of the kindergarten year, children involved in such a program are usually ready to begin writing their own "stories," not with perfect spelling and grammar, which come later, but with excitement and growing confidence in their power to use language to describe their own experience.

In a small number of kindergartens, teachers ask children to begin "writing" their own pieces from the very beginning of the year. Such writing tends to make great use of drawing, to use pho- netic, or "private" spelling, and to range from picture labels to fairly detailed stories. In the hands of a skillful teacher, however, such writing is a useful learning activity and a powerful motiva- tional device. With encouragement, children love to write, espe- cially about topics that they choose themselves. It's fun telling about things that you know, and it feels good when people praise what you've done. What professional writers wouldn't want to know that they would always have a proud and appreciative audi- ence? If your kindergarten child is lucky enough to have a teacher who gets her children to write, be thankful and supportive. Don't spoil things by worrying about spelling. The teacher is not an idiot; she knows that, eventually, spelling counts. But what counts right now is that the child continue to increase his language power and his confidence in using it in all its forms—listening, speaking, reading, and writing.

(Some kindergartens also conduct formal beginning reading instruction for children who are ready for it. Since most children do not begin such instruction until first grade, our account of such instruction appears in the chapter "Reading in the First Grade, p. 84.)

WHAT TO LOOK FOR IN A GOOD KINDERGARTEN LANGUAGE PROGRAM

Most parents cannot expect to be experts about teaching language skills in the kindergarten. However, every parent can tell whether certain key qualities of a good language program are present or absent. If the answers to most or all of the following questions are yes, chances are your child is participating in an effective program. If many of the answers are no, you may want to inquire further by talking with your child's teacher and, possibly, the principal.

What to Look for in the Classroom

When you visit your child's classroom, do you see

- Interesting centers of activity, with many things to work with (for example, animals, plants, painting materials, paper, and crayons)?
- Many attractive books, stored so that children may use them when they wish?
- Paintings and drawings that remind the children of things they have done and learned?
- Printed captions on objects, naming the objects with words children know?
- Charts with letters of the alphabet, once children have been introduced to them?
- Children's printed names on the paintings or drawings they have made, displayed about the room?
- Displays of children's stories, as children dictate them to the teacher?
- Displays of pictures and stories the children have written themselves?

What to Look for From Your Child

As the kindergarten year progresses, does your child

- Bring home things he made in school that develop visual and motor readiness skills?
- Bring home worksheets that practice reading/writing readiness skills?
- Bring home paintings, drawings, and stories he has made or written?
- Discuss freely "what they did today"?
- Remember stories or poems the teacher read?
- Begin to look for letters and written words at home (later in the year)?
- Begin to recognize written words on cereal boxes, in magazines, or in books you read to him?
- Show a sense of excitement and confidence about speaking, reading, and writing?

What to Look for From the Teacher

When you talk to your child's teacher, does she

- Describe clearly what the class has been doing and what she plans for it to do?
- Explain clearly why the children made the things they bring home?
- Know your child's individual interests and abilities—for example, does she know what your child reads and writes at home?
- Show you examples of your child's recent pictures or written work?
- Tell you what stories or poems she has been reading to the class?
- Suggest stories or poems for you to read to your child at home?

HOW TO HELP YOUR CHILD AT HOME

Ideally, the kindergarten child should live in one world. Home and school should not be totally separate from each other. The activity and values in the one should reinforce the activity and values in the other.

The following is a list of ways you can help your child at home to develop the language capacity he is working on at school. The exact form and length of these activities depend upon your child's individual maturity and your own patience and skill.

Do's

- Praise and encourage your child's every effort to speak well, to read, and to write.
- Read to your child, every day if possible. Read classic children's books, current children's books, poems, rhymes. If you temporarily run out of material, make up stories or read from the newspaper. But read.
- Relate some of your reading to the child's interest—policemen, dinosaurs, airplanes.
- Get your child to retell stories he has been told.
- Let your child see you reading and writing. Activity is important when parents do it.
- Give your child lots of books to look at himself: picture books, storybooks, books that he can "read" and books that you read to him. If you can't afford to buy many books, get them from the library. (Take your child with you and let him help to choose what books to bring home.)
- Encourage your child to draw pictures and talk about them. Let him label the pictures with his own words and letters, even if you can't recognize them.
- Give your child lots of records to listen to—stories and poems as well as music.

- Encourage your child to watch *Sesame Street* and similar television programs. Watch television together and talk about it afterward.
- Talk to your child often—about family events, trips, television programs, the weather, games, friends. Ask him questions that lead him to describe and think about his experience.
- Give your child frequent opportunities to express opinions and make choices. ("What is your favorite color?" "Which piece would you like, the larger one or the smaller one?")
- Ask your child about school. Be interested and specific. (Go beyond "What did you do today?" to "Did the egg hatch yet? Who fed the chickens today? What did you do that you liked best?")
- Play word games with your child. (Say a sentence and let your child supply the last word: "If we drop the dish on the floor it will _____." Or say, "I'm thinking of something in this room that is *red*," and let your child name all the red objects until he names the one you had in mind. Then let *him* think of an object of a certain color, and you name all the objects of that color until you guess the one he has in mind.
- Refer to objects by color and shape. ("Please bring me the *red* box in the bedroom." "Where did we put the *round* ball that we play with?")
- Give your child directions involving two or three steps and ask him to listen and follow them. ("Please, go to the kitchen, open the cabinet, and bring me the brush.")
- Ask your child to point out color, shapes, or letters that look the same.
- Encourage your child to print his name and any other words that he may know.

Don'ts

- Don't expect too much. Remember that children develop at different rates. It is not important that your child learn to read and write yet. Your job, at present, is to make him feel loved and successful.
- Don't persist with an activity if your child becomes frustrated or inattentive. Remember, this is not the time for hitting the books. Your child is still in kindergarten.
- Don't criticize your child. If he can't make errors now—at kindergarten age, with you, at home—then when can he? This is not an age for developing perfection. It is a time for building confidence.
- Don't criticize your child's teacher. If you are concerned about what the teacher is or isn't doing, talk to her or, if necessary, to the principal. At this young age, children learn better when they feel positive about their teachers. Don't destroy your child's confidence in the teacher and in the work he is doing by criticizing the teacher in front of him.

Mathematics in the Kindergarten

SOME BASIC IDEAS ABOUT MATHEMATICS

If the use of language is our most distinctly human activity, the language of mathematics is one of our most distinctly human achievements. Prehistoric and pre-mathematical man lived at the mercy of mysterious forces difficult to predict and impossible to control. For there to be trade, for man to be able to measure time and distance, for the force of gravity, the size of the universe, and the structure of the atom to be understood, mathematics was a necessity. And what a wonderfully human invention! For mathematics does not exist outside the human minds, which see the patterns and create the relationships that it describes. We would not have our civilization without it, and yet it is truly a case of "mind over matter"!

That your child acquire a solid knowledge of mathematics is of utmost importance. In tomorrow's world, even more than in today's, those who are mathematically uncomfortable or inept will be sorely handicapped. Not only will rudimentary math continue to be needed in daily living, but as technology becomes increasingly complex, more and more jobs will require mathematical knowledge; even if computers are programmed by the few to do the work of the many, you may wish your child to be among the few.

Fortunately, almost all children can master mathematical fundamentals, and most can eventually attain relatively sophisticated proficiency. All that is required is good teaching, the encouragement of parents, and your child's developing confidence in the use of his mind.

Good elementary-school mathematics programs reflect certain ideas about the nature of mathematics.

1. *Mathematics is more than arithmetic.* Granted, even in the computer age, it is still important that your child learn to add, subtract, multiply, and divide. But such learning by itself is not enough. Children must also learn the elements of geometry, the skills of estimation and measurement, the use of probability and statistics, and the concept of function. Such learning should begin early, since it flows naturally out of children's experience if taught well in an encouraging atmosphere. The kindergarten child whose teacher helps the class chart, or *graph*, the number of children who have birthdays month by month is acquiring useful mathematical knowledge about categories, order, symbolic representation, and so on.

2. *Mathematics is related to experience.* As adults, we tend to think of mathematics as an abstract world sufficient unto itself. And indeed, an understanding of the unity and coherence of certain mathematical systems—Euclidean geometry, for example—is essential for the more mature student. But for young children, as for primitive man, mathematics is a way of quantifying and understanding relationships between real things, space, and time. The symbols and abstractions themselves make no sense unless they are rooted in the child's experience.

3. *The essence of mathematics is problem solving.* As Stephen Willoughby wrote in a paper for the Council for Basic Education in Washington, D.C., "The main purpose of teaching mathematics is

to educate people to use mathematical thought to solve real problems." At bottom, mathematics is an activity of the mind. It is not enough to memorize the formulas or to be able to follow the established procedures (called algorithms in some schools) to get an accurate answer. What is important is to be able to use the power of mathematical thinking to bring greater clarity or order to experience. Whether one is Einstein discerning the relationship between matter and energy or the small child figuring out how to divide the birthday cake, the trick is to use one's mind in a mathematical fashion to solve the problem at hand.

These basic ideas characterize good mathematics programs throughout the grades, the kindergarten included. Children at this level should begin to experience many mathematical ideas and forms, should build upon their concrete experience to develop conceptual thinking, and should use their minds to solve problems that have meaning for them. How do kindergarten teachers teach these things? What are the specific goals and methods of the kindergarten mathematics program?

Kindergartens throughout the United States vary in what mathematics they teach and how much. In many programs, the goals are limited to counting objects, recognizing written numbers, and learning basic geometric shapes, such as squares, circles, and triangles. In some, children are introduced to the concept of sets (groups of related objects) and actually begin to learn the fundamentals of arithmetic. In the authors' view, it probably does not matter how *much* formal math your child learns at this age. Unless your child is truly precocious, there will be plenty of time for advanced study later on. (No one was ever deprived of the chance to take calculus in high school because of a limited kindergarten program.)

What does matter is the *quality* of your child's experience with mathematics. Many children have been blocked from studying math because they have been made to feel that it is dull or hard or not for them. Boys and girls both should be helped to develop an attitude that math is fun, that it makes sense, and that they can do it. However much or little math your child may do in school, he should like it and feel comfortable with it. Above all, your child should experience the pleasure and excitement of using his mind.

THE MATHEMATICS CURRICULUM

Most contemporary mathematics curricula contain five parts, or *strands* (as they are sometimes called):

Numbers and numeration
Operations with whole numbers
Operations with fractions
Probability and statistics
Geometry and measurement

Some schools do more than others with this curriculum, but few, if any, go beyond it. Some schools include a sixth part, problem solving. In the authors' view, however, problem solving is the goal of all mathematics and should be incorporated into the teaching and learning of each part of the curriculum. We shall discuss word problems and several problem-solving skills later in this book.

These five main parts of the mathematics curriculum are taught throughout the elementary grades. At the kindergarten level, the skills and knowledge that children should acquire are as follows.

Numbers and Numeration

- Sorting and classifying: Sort and classify concrete objects such as blocks, buttons, and bottle tops. Explore likenesses and differences of color, shape, size, material.

- Sets: Use the word *set* synonymously with words like *group, lot, pile, bunch,* and *heap.*
- Equality, inequality: Compare sets with *more, less,* and *the same* amounts. Make comparisons and learn such terms as *bigger than, greater than, less than, same size as,* and *equal to.*
- Counting—cardinal numbers: Learn to use the cardinal numbers 1–20. Count the items in a set and understand that the last number counted in a set tells how many items are in that set.
- One-to-one correspondence: Learn that if two sets can be matched (one item in set *B* for each item in set *A*), they have the same cardinal number.
- Conservation: Learn that the number of a set remains the same no matter how the elements are arranged; for example, if there are six blocks in a set, the number remains six whether the blocks are placed in a row or stacked in a pile.
- Order: Order sets of objects from smallest to largest and from largest to smallest. Learn the idea of *first, last,* and *middle.*
- Counting—ordinal numbers: Learn to use ordinal number names from *first* through *ninth.*
- Numerals: Observe numerals (symbols for numbers) in the environment. Proceed gradually from handling concrete objects to using pictures to using written numerals. Develop the ability to read and write numerals from at least 0 to 10.

Operations With Whole Numbers

- Grouping: Group objects by twos, threes, fives.
- Combining: Put two sets together to produce a new set. Count the number of the new set.
- Sharing: Share sets of objects (cookies, toys, crayons). Remove items from a set ("all the blue ones" or "all the broken ones").
- Sequence: Learn the idea of *one more* by adding items to a set. Count the new numbers. Learn the ideas of *before, after,* and *between.*

Operations With Fractions

- Inequality: Learn through work with concrete objects such ideas as "a whole is *more than* a half" and "a half is *less than* a whole."
- Two equal parts of a whole: Learn the idea of *half* through work with concrete objects. Learn that two halves make a whole.
- Many equal parts of a whole: Learn through sharing experiences that a whole, such as a cake or an apple, may be divided into many equal parts. Learn the words *thirds* and *fourths*.
- Many equal parts of a set: Learn through sharing experiences that sets of objects, such as a bag of marbles or a pile of blocks, can be divided into two or more equal parts. Learn that the total number of objects is unchanged.

Probability and Statistics

- Sorting and classifying: Sort and classify concrete objects by color, shape, size, material, and other properties. Learn to use two categories at a time.
- Equality and inequality: Compare items in terms of *more, less,* and *the same amount*.
- Concrete graphs: Pile blocks in two stacks to represent children who prefer apple or grape juice, cookies or crackers.
- Representational graphs: Discuss graphs such as the one in Figure 1.
- Estimation: Participate in activities that involve anticipating outcomes, such as guessing how many blocks can be stacked before the pile falls or whether a bean bag will land on number 3.

Figure 1. How Do We Get to School?

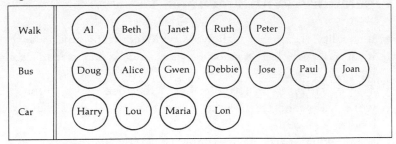

Geometry and Measurement

- Comparing size and distance: Compare the length, width, and depth of objects. Use terms like *longer than, taller than, smaller than, shorter than,* and *as long as.* Compare distances. Use terms like *farther than* and *nearer than.*
- Mass: Weigh objects, first in the hands and then on balance scales. Use terms such as *heavier than* and *lighter than.*
- Capacity: Use sand, water, beans, and the like to compare the capacity of containers. Use terms such as *holds more than, holds less than,* and *holds the same amount.*
- Temperature: Compare the temperatures of the weather or of objects in general terms, such as *cooler than, hotter than,* and *as cold as.*
- Time: Compare the length of events, like story time or snack time, using estimation or rough instruments, such as egg timers or an hourglass. Use terms such as *longer, shorter,* and *as long as.*
- Nonstandard units of measurement: Use nonstandard units of measurement, such as blocks or children's feet for distance, buttons or bottle tops for weight, cupfuls or bowlfuls for capacity, and faucet drips for time.
- Money: Use real money for activities such as shopping. Learn the names of bills and coins.
- Shape: Observe geometric shapes in the environment and learn to use their names: squares, rectangles, circles, triangles. Count the faces, edges, and corners on three-dimensional objects.

• Patterns: Create geometric shapes and designs with blocks and paper.

TEACHING THE MATHEMATICS CURRICULUM

How do kindergarten teachers help children learn these mathematics skills and knowledge? In the section "Reading/Writing Readiness Skills" we saw that in a well-run kindergarten most of the activity, as well as the physical environment of the classroom, contributes to language learning. So it is with mathematics. Kindergarten teachers do teach mathematics lessons to small groups and to the total class, as we shall see. But much of the teaching and learning is informal, a natural outgrowth of an activity that the child regards as play or as part of classroom routine. Consider these examples.

A brisk October morning. The teacher is sitting on a small chair near the middle of the room; the children are seated on the floor around her. One child takes attendance. He walks around the circle, counting each child as he goes. When he has trouble or skips a number, the teacher helps. He finishes at twenty-three. The teacher asks, "How many children in the class?"

The children answer, "Twenty-four."

"Who's missing?" she asks. The attendance taker says, "Larry."

"You may go to the office and tell Mrs. Lee that Larry is absent."

A dreary December day. Snack time. The teacher and two child helpers are about to give out milk or juice and cookies. The class has come to order on the floor. The teacher asks, "How many want milk?" The helpers count the hands. The teacher says, "Let's make a chart." On the bulletin board, under the picture of a milk bottle and the word *Milk*, she places the name cards of the children who want milk. "How many want juice?" The helpers count, and under a picture of an orange and the words *Orange Juice* the teacher places the name cards of the children who want juice. "Do more people want milk or do more people want juice?" the teacher asks.

"Milk," say the children. The helpers give out the cookies, two to each child.

About an hour before lunch on a raw day in March. An adult volunteer and four children—two boys and two girls—are baking cookies. The adult fills a measuring cup with flour and a child pours it into the bowl. "We need three cups," she says. "How much flour do we put into the cup this time?"

"Up to the top," says a child. The others agree.

"Is that the same or not as much as the first time?" she asks.

"The same," they say. They fill the cup and pour the contents into the bowl.

"How many more cups do we need?" she asks.

"One more," they say.

Early afternoon on an April day. A girl is in the block corner, building a wall around a stuffed animal. The wall is patterned, vertical rectangles alternating with horizontal rectangles. There are not enough rectangles to close the wall. The teacher watches silently. The girl begins to turn away. The teacher holds up a square and asks, "How many of these do you need to make one of those [rectangles]?" The girl puts the squares together and finishes her enclosure.

In situations of this kind, the role of the teacher is to observe the manner in which a child approaches an activity, to listen to children's conversations about what each is doing, and to be alert for the right moment to ask the question that will help the child to think and to expand his understanding. Because children of this age learn through playing, the teacher creates the "play" situation and then helps children work within it to acquire skills and knowledge. The method has been called *planned serendipity*.

As the kindergarten year progresses, more and more often the teacher will call the whole class or a small group together for a more formal lesson.

A morning in early October. A lesson about triangles is under way. The teacher sits in front of the class and shows a chart with the shapes of a circle, a square, a rectangle, and a triangle. Each has a different color. The teacher points to the square and asks, "Who remembers the name of this shape?" The children answer. "And this one?" pointing to the rectangle. The teacher and the children review the differences between the two shapes. They have worked on these shapes before. Now the teacher points to the triangle. "Who knows what this is?" Some of the children already know its name. The teacher names it, too. She and the children count the sides of the triangle. They count the sides of the square and the rectangle. They discuss how the triangle is different from the other two shapes. "What picture might you draw that would have a triangle in it?" asks the teacher.

"A house," a child answers. They continue talking about objects they could draw that would have triangles in them. The teacher gives out paper and cardboard triangles. She tells the children to make a picture with a triangle in it. They may use the cardboard shape for tracing. The teacher circulates, helping and encouraging the children.

Mid-morning on a bright May day. The children are sitting at tables in small groups. They have cut-out paper pennies and nickels before them. The teacher is standing in front of them with the blackboard behind her. She has some real coins in an egg crate and explains that for the morning's lesson the paper coins will be used to take the place of the real coins.

"What is this?" she asks holding up a paper penny.

"A penny," a boy at the far table responds.

"What's another word for a penny?" the teacher questions.

"A cent," answers a little girl.

"Good work," praises the teacher. "Soon we're going to be so sure of our money, we'll be able to work well in our store." Off to a side of the room is a large cardboard play store that the children have built and painted with the teacher's help.

The teacher continues, "I'm going to write a number on the board. I'd like you to count the pennies until you have the same number of pennies in your hand as the number I write on the board."

The children follow instructions while the teacher goes from child to child, helping those who need help, encouraging the unsure, and praising those who have completed the task.

The lesson moves on. "Look for the large silver coin, not the small. Who can tell me what we call the large silver coin?"

"A nickel," cries a boy eagerly.

"And another name for it?"

"Five cents," responds a girl in front of the teacher.

The teacher puts a paper nickel in one hand and five cents in another and tells the children to do the same. "The nickel feels different from the five pennies, but it's worth just the same. If you were buying gum and it cost five cents or a nickel, the way it did when I was little, you could pay for it with either the nickel or the five cents."

The lesson over, the children put the paper coins away in their folders and get ready for snack.

All of these learning activities—the informal and the formal—follow certain principles. First, they begin with concrete physical experience. Children handle blocks, chips, coins, buttons, or other objects and base their ideas about mathematics upon their operation with these concrete objects. (Remember that children of this age are typically in Piaget's pre-operational stage.) Gradually they progress from actual objects to pictures of these objects, and only then from pictures to numerals. You may hear teachers speak of *manipulative materials* in the math program. Don't be put off by the jargon. Be glad that they know enough to use real objects to give your child a solid grounding in learning math.

Second, children learn their math through real-life and play situations as well as through formal lessons. They experience math as something that helps them to solve problems in these situations.

Third, the emphasis is on understanding mathematical ideas and relationships. There is a place for rote learning, but it comes later in children's development, not in kindergarten.

Fourth, the teacher provides many kinds of activities in many settings. Children learn at different rates and in different ways, and it is important that each child be helped to find a way to be successful.

Fifth, the experiences are repetitive. Good teachers know that skills and knowledge gained earlier must be reviewed and reinforced if children are truly to master them.

Sixth, the experiences are cumulative. Good teachers help children build upon what they already know to acquire new skills and understanding.

Finally, in the best kindergarten, children are constantly challenged to think—to use their minds logically and with imagination. As we have said, mathematics is not just a set of facts to memorize—it is an activity of mind.

WHAT TO LOOK FOR IN A GOOD KINDERGARTEN MATH PROGRAM

As we said about the language program, most parents cannot be experts on teaching mathematics in the kindergarten. However, every parent can tell whether certain key signs of a good math program are present or absent. If the answers to most or all of the following questions are yes, chances are your child is participating in an effective program. If many of the answers are no, you may want to inquire further by talking with your child's teacher and, possibly, the principal.

What to Look for in a Classroom

When you visit your child's classroom, do you see

- Blocks, bottle caps, or other objects for counting and sorting?
- A corner or center for block building?
- Informal graphs on posterboard, on the blackboard, or on the bulletin board showing birthdays, the kinds of juice children like, the color hair they have, and so on?
- Pictures or cutouts of geometric shapes, such as circles, squares, triangles, and rectangles?
- Number charts (later in the year)?

What to Look for From Your Child

As the kindergarten year progresses, does your child

- Describe activities involving measurement and estimation?
- Understand words like *first, last, next, more than,* and *less than?*
- Begin to look for written numbers on signs, in magazines and newspapers, on television?
- Begin to understand the relative value of coins and dollar bills?
- Show a sense of excitement and confidence in using his mind about numbers?

What to Look for From the Teacher

When you talk to your child's kindergarten teacher, does she

- Describe clearly what the class has been doing in mathematics and what she plans for it to do?

- Know your child's individual abilities and feelings about mathematics?
- Show you examples of work your child has done involving mathematics?
- Suggest activities for you and your child to do at home?

HOW TO HELP YOUR CHILD AT HOME

With a little thoughtful attention you can reinforce at home what your child is learning about mathematics at school. But remember, patience is more important than skill. Be interested, be positive, be cheerful. Unless you can sustain a supportive attitude, leave matters to your child and to his teacher.

Do's

- Praise and encourage your child's efforts to "use mathematics"—to count, to estimate, to measure, to use numbers.
- Give your child blocks to play with, preferably of the "unit" sort (the sizes are interrelated, for example, 1/2/4).
- Use expressions like *bigger than, smaller than,* and *the same amount.*"
- Use numbers when playing with your child. ("Let's each take six pieces.")
- Help your child to use coins and to begin to make change.
- Talk with your child about the numbered days on the calendar.
- Point out written numbers in common use, such as house numbers, numbers on the television set, on clocks, on the school bus, and on sports uniforms.
- Help your child begin to tell time, on both digital and analog clocks.
- Encourage your child to write numbers.

Don'ts

- Don't be impatient. Remember that your child must develop mentally to understand math and that children develop at different rates. Your child's apparent difficulty is more likely due to slow development than to deficient intelligence. Besides, who ever did better with an anxious and disapproving parent looking over his or her shoulder?
- Don't persist with an activity or game if your child becomes frustrated or inattentive. Kindergarten children's attention span is short. What you want for your child at this age is happy success, not weary perseverance.
- Don't say that you (or some people) are just "no good at math." No one of normal intelligence needs to be "no good at math" unless he is made to think he is. Praise and encourage your child's efforts and don't give him an easy out.
- Don't criticize or belittle the work your child is doing. If it seems too easy for you, try to remember that you're not the one in kindergarten.

THE SIGNS OF PROGRESS

By the time they leave kindergarten, children who are making normal progress in mathematics should be able to do the following.

Spatial Relationships

- Distinguish between *up/down, top/bottom, front/back, over/under, in/out, on/off, left/right.*
- Demonstrate an understanding of concepts like *next to, beside,* and *between.*

- Distinguish between degrees of size: *large/larger/largest, small/smaller/smallest.*
- Arrange sets of objects from smallest to largest, largest to smallest.
- Identify and form common two-dimensional shapes, such as circles, triangles, squares, and rectangles.
- Identify and form patterns of common shapes.
- Identify common three-dimensional shapes, such as balls, cubes, and boxes.
- Recognize and count the faces, edges, and corners of three-dimensional shapes.

Measurement

- Distinguish between objects that are *bigger than/smaller than/as big as, taller than/shorter than/as tall as.*
- Distinguish between *farther/nearer* (closer) when referring to distance.
- Distinguish between *heavier than/lighter than/the same weight as.*
- Distinguish between *hotter than/cooler than/just as hot as* (or *just as cold as*).
- Distinguish between *full/empty, more than/less than,* when referring to the contents of containers.

Time

- Recognize the times of the day: morning, noon, afternoon, and night.
- Distinguish between *before/after, early/late, younger/older.*
- Distinguish between *longer than/shorter than/as long as* when referring to time.
- Tell time to the hour on analog and digital clocks.

Money

- Identify common coins: penny, nickel, dime, and quarter.

Numbers in the Environment

- Recite personal data, such as age, birthday, address, and telephone number.
- Identify numerals on common objects, such as house numbers, room numbers, and numbers on television sets, clocks, buses, auditorium seats.

Numerals and Numbers

- Count and write the cardinal numbers 1–10.
- Count the number of objects in a set of up to ten objects.
- Count the ordinal numbers first through tenth.
- Match the ordinal numbers first through tenth to the cardinal numbers 1–10.
- Identify the ordinal position of each object in a row through ten objects.
- Construct a number line from one to ten.
- Count forward and backward on the number line.

By the time they leave kindergarten, many children will have mastered the skills listed above. In addition, they will be able to do the following.

Sets

- Demonstrate understanding that a set is a group of related objects.

- Distinguish between *all/none/some* of the objects in a set.
- Count the number of objects in a set (up to twenty).
- Demonstrate understanding that the number of objects in a set does not change when the objects are rearranged.
- Compare two sets by matching which has more or fewer.
- Compare two sets by matching and showing the same number.
- Recognize that when one more object is added, the resulting set is larger than the original set.
- Recognize that when one object is removed (subtracted), the resulting set is smaller than the original set.

More Numerals and Numbers

- Associate the numerals 1 through 20 with a set having one through twenty objects.
- Recognize the symbols 1 through 20 as numerals for the numbers one through twenty.
- Write the numerals 1 through 20.
- Associate the numeral 0 with a set having no objects.
- Recognize the symbol 0 as a numeral for the number zero.
- Write the numeral 0.

Fractions

- Distinguish part of a unit from the whole unit.
- Distinguish part of a set from the whole set.
- Recognize equal parts of a whole, and identify each equal part as half of the whole.
- Divide objects and sets into equal parts (halves).
- Recognize that a whole object or set is greater than one half of the object or set, and vice versa.
- Recognize that when two halves are joined, the whole object or set is restored.

Graphs

- Construct and interpret concrete graphs using blocks, cubes, macaroni, and so on.
- Construct and interpret simple pictorial graphs representing number relationships.
- Match the number of units on a graph to the number of objects under consideration.
- Write the numeral that represents the number of units in the graph (up to 20).

Social Studies in the Kindergarten

THE SOCIAL STUDIES CURRICULUM

The kindergarten social studies program grows seamlessly out of the nature of the child and the structure of the classroom. The typical child entering kindergarten arrives at school preoccupied with himself and the close world of his family. Although eager to learn, he may still have difficulty taking the perspective of others. Although he has had some experiences outside his home, his understanding of how people live and work with one another in the larger world is limited.

The good kindergarten teacher helps the child to realize that he is both unique and similar to others. She helps him acquire the skills necessary for cooperative work and play with others. And she leads him to a widening understanding of how individuals and groups live and work in the larger community.

Much of this teaching occurs naturally as an outcome of classroom routines. Children must learn to share toys, to take turns, to listen to adults and to one another, and to respect adult authority. All of these are social skills that are required for civilized life within and beyond the classroom.

Some of the teaching is more direct, as when the teacher reads stories about children who live in other places and other times and has the class talk about how they are the same or different. (Even here, it is hard to tell what is "social studies" and what is "literature.") The social studies textbooks in widespread use in American classrooms vary in their content and organization. In general, however, there is a progression from an emphasis on the child himself in kindergarten ("Myself," "Me," "Here We Are") to the family in the first grade ("Family," "Living in Families," "People") to the community in the second grade ("Communities," "Groups and Communities," "Living in Communities"). You should not be surprised or upset if the content of your child's social studies program in these early grades is different from another child's in another classroom. Across the country there is no consensus about what a good social studies program should contain. What is important is that your child learn the skills and attitudes of constructive social behavior and that he begin to understand how people live and work in the world beyond his own personal circle.

TEACHING THE KINDERGARTEN SOCIAL STUDIES CURRICULUM

Teachers approach the social studies curriculum in a thousand different ways. They ask children to talk about themselves while other children listen: "What is your name?" "Where do you live?" "Whom do you live with?" "What do you like to do best?" "What is your favorite food?" "How are you different from others?" "How are you the same?" They read stories about other children and families, and discuss similarities and differences. They have children look at baby pictures and laugh at how they have changed. They have them make cutouts of the outlines of their hands or bodies on construction paper. Later, the focus shifts toward others. They talk about holidays and their meaning, and they read holiday books. Children paint holiday pictures, make a myriad of holiday posters, murals, greeting cards, gifts. They talk about the other adults in the school—the principal, the nurse, the secretary, the custodian, the bus driver—and they discuss what they do. Gradually, the child's world enlarges.

By the spring of the kindergarten year, children may be ready for a more sustained activity, as for example, a visit to the local supermarket. In the days before the visit, the teacher leads discussions about what children have seen there on previous trips with their parents, grandparents, or baby-sitter. They talk about their favorite foods, about how the food gets to the store, about who the people are who work there and what they do. Most of the children have handled small amounts of money and made some purchases of their own. All have seen products advertised on television; they talk about where these products can be purchased and whether they cost much or little.

When the class visits the store, they look for their favorite foods, for products that are familiar to them, for things they did not expect to find. They talk to the cashier, to the meat cutter, to the manager, and find out what they do. They purchase what they had agreed on in advance, and watch the process of exchanging money for goods and of making change.

Back in the classroom, during the next few days, they build their own store in the block corner, their own kitchen in the doll corner. They play with empty food boxes and cans, with play money, with a cash register. They make price signs and advertising posters. They take turns acting out the various roles: customer, manager, cashier, produce clerk. They talk about their experience with the teacher and with one another. The teacher writes down what they say and tacks the stories on the bulletin board. Some children write and illustrate their own stories, and these, too, are displayed.

What do the children learn from this experience? From their

point of view, they learn about the store and how it works—important knowledge for healthy young people who take a keen interest in the food they eat and in the way the world works to bring it to their table. From an adult point of view, we can see that they are learning

- Language arts, as they expand their vocabularies about the store and its contents and as they speak and write about it.
- Mathematics, as they count items, weigh produce, determine prices, make change.
- Science, as they explore what is frozen and what is not and what happens if things thaw, or as they compare what is fresh and what is not and begin to investigate why.
- Social studies, as they grasp the concepts of consumer and producer, of money and prices, of the way people work with one another to make life possible in our society.

WHAT TO LOOK FOR IN A GOOD KINDERGARTEN SOCIAL STUDIES PROGRAM

Again, the specific content of the kindergarten social studies program is not important. What matters is that your child learn the skills and attitudes of constructive social behavior and that he begin to understand how people live and work in the world beyond his own personal circle. Here are some signs of progress to look for:

- Does the teacher say your child adapts well to classroom rules and routines, for example, sharing, taking turns, and so on?
- Does the teacher say your child enjoys playing with other children—one at a time, in a group?

- Does the teacher say your child functions well in a group?
- Does your child show curiosity about your family—who your relatives are, where you used to live, what work you do?
- Does your child show curiosity about the people who have special roles in the community—the people who deliver the mail, collect the trash, drive the fire truck?
- Does your child bring home stories or pictures, or objects he's made, that reflect social studies activity, for example, materials relating to a current holiday?

If the answers to questions like these are yes, as they are likely to be, your child is making normal progress. If the answers are no, you should make an appointment to see your child's teacher to get more information on what your child's problems of growth and adjustment may be.

Science in the Kindergarten

THE SCIENCE CURRICULUM

The kindergarten child is a scientist by nature. He is unfailingly curious about his environment, eager to explore, delighted by discovery. He is fascinated by new objects, new life, new events. He uses each of his senses—sight, hearing, smell, touch, taste—to savor the essence of each new experience. He is not content just to talk and listen; he wants to handle, smell, turn upside down, take apart, inspect. His mind is ever active, with an eye for detail ("Why doesn't the rain run straight down the window?") and a sense of the cosmic ("What holds the moon up in the sky?"). Like the adult scientist who has retained his childhood curiosity, above all else he wishes to *know*.

The task of the kindergarten science program is to nourish this curiosity. Later in the grades there will be time for the formal scientific method and an organized body of science content. For now, the teacher should involve your child with animals, plants, the weather, rocks, leaves, shells, magnets—whatever triggers the child's curiosity and sets him to exploring. She should answer his countless questions ("Snow is water that freezes in the cold air before it hits the ground"), and she should ask other questions to prompt new investigations ("What do you think might happen if we bring some snow inside?"). As with most of the kindergarten curriculum, good science at this level means nurturing the child's instinct to explore the world around him.

TEACHING THE KINDERGARTEN SCIENCE CURRICULUM

As with social studies, teachers approach the kindergarten science curriculum in a thousand different ways. Children bring animals to the classroom—chickens, rats, hamsters, gerbils, kittens, snakes, turtles, frogs—and they feed them, water them, clean them, watch them change and grow. They grow their own plants from seeds or bulbs and watch what happens when a plant is left in the dark, when it is put outdoors, when it has too much or too little water. They observe the effects of sun, water, different soils, fertilizer. They walk in the woods and inspect the trees, the rotting branches, the moss, the sapling reaching for a place in the sun. They bring in bark and leaves, and compare shape, color, texture, smell. They keep track of the weather—good days, rainy days, hot days, cold days, windy days—and they record, with the teacher's help, the temperature, the direction of the wind, whether the flag blew straight out or hung down. They put water outside to see if it freezes, and they bring it in again to watch it thaw. They look for the moon in the daytime sky, and they watch for where it is and how it looks before they go to bed at night.

All of this activity with the natural world serves more than one purpose. Important as it is in its own right, it is also a springboard for talking and "writing," a motivation for reading and painting, a chance to sort objects and perhaps count them, an opportunity for working together and taking turns. Thus, science and language and math and social studies and the arts are all involved, each informing the other and all helping the child to understand his world. Would that this unity of knowledge were so easy to sustain as the child progresses through the grades!

WHAT TO LOOK FOR IN A GOOD KINDERGARTEN SCIENCE PROGRAM

The specific content of the kindergarten science program is not important. What matters is that your child be stimulated and encouraged to use his mind and senses to explore the natural world around him and as much of it as can be brought into the classroom. Here are some things you might look for:

- Are there animals in the classroom? If not, will there be?
- Is your child allowed to help care for the animals?
- Are there plants in the classroom? Is your child allowed to experiment with them?
- Is your child encouraged to handle the things he is investigating, or does he just look and listen?
- Does your child tell you about interesting objects or events he has seen in school?
- Does your child show curiosity about his natural environment at home and when you travel—about animals, plants, the weather, electricity, rocks, the ocean, whatever?
- Does your child feel good about using his mind and senses to explore new experiences?
- Does your child bring home stories or pictures, or objects he's made, that reflect science activity, such as pictures or stories of leaves falling in the autumn?

If the answers to questions like these are yes, chances are your child is placed with a good teacher of science in the kindergarten. If the answers are no, you may wish to enrich your child's experiences at home. Here are two books that contain some imaginative ideas: *Off to a Good Start* (New York: Amy L. Toole & Ellen Boehm, Walker, 1983) and *Preparing Young Children for Science* (New York: Lois Arnold, Schocken Books, 1980).

FIRST GRADE

The First-Grade Child as a Learner

The typical first-grade child is six years old. Within the past year he has changed greatly. He is more developed physically and neurologically, and he has a better developed sense of self. Although he still loves his parents and remains dependent on them, he is more aware of himself as a separate person who functions independently in the world outside the family. He is more aware of the world beyond the home. He has a better sense of time past and time future, and lives less in the here and now. He has friends his own age, and they are important to him.

Intellectually, the first-grade child is nearing the end of Piaget's pre-operational stage and approaching the stage of concrete operations. His capacity to use language has grown tremendously. He is much more able to see things from another person's point of view. He is able to tell that the shape of a container does not determine how much it holds, and that six blocks are six blocks no matter how they are arranged.

Above all, he is ready and eager to use his mind. He loves to count and spell. He loves to learn new facts. He loves learning games and puzzles. He loves to talk about what he is learning.

Most first-grade children have attended kindergarten or some other preschool program. They have learned to get along in a group, and they are more able than they were to sit still and focus on a learning task. They are ready for formal instruction.

Reading in the First Grade

THE IMPORTANCE OF READING

"Reading is a basic life skill. It is a cornerstone for a child's success in school and, indeed, throughout life. Without the ability to read well, opportunities for personal fulfillment and job success inevitably will be lost." So says *Becoming a Nation of Readers*, a report of the Commission on Reading, published in 1985. Even in the age of television and computers, your child's skill and fluency in reading may determine his life's chances. And for most children, the time and place to begin formal instruction in reading is in first grade.

If your child is lucky, he comes from a home in which he has been immersed in the spoken and written word. You and other family members have read to him often; you have given him books of his own to look at and to "read"; you talk with him constantly and encourage his growing ability to express himself with words. Perhaps your child has attended a kindergarten program such as that described earlier. There he developed many of the reading readiness skills, such as those of auditory and visual discrimination. Perhaps he even began to read a little. Or perhaps your child is less developmentally ready. No matter what his background, however, once he enters first grade, he will be involved in the process of learning to read. For first-grade children throughout our society, the motto is, "Ready or not, here I come."

WHAT IS READING?

As a practical matter, we all know what reading is. We certainly know the difference between a person who can read and a person who cannot. For teachers, however, a definition is important, because the way one thinks about reading influences the way one tries to teach it. Most contemporary experts agree with the Commission on Reading that "reading is the process of constructing meaning from written texts." The ability to sound out letters and to recognize words is a necessary but not sufficient condition. True reading involves comprehending the meaning of the text and relating it to what the reader already knows. The young child who recites the words while the parent turns the pages of a familiar storybook is not really reading; he is repeating from memory what he has often heard. The person who is able to pronounce the printed words but cannot understand their meaning is not reading either, any more than when we pronounce words in a foreign language we do not know.

Seen from this point of view, reading involves both *word recognition* skills and *comprehension* skills. It is a complex task requiring the integration of many subskills and sources of information.

HOW DO CHILDREN LEARN TO READ?

Before we begin our discussion, it may be reassuring to remember that most people do learn to read. Educators may not be able to describe exactly what children have to learn to do in order to read. But just as almost all children develop the miraculous ability to speak—without benefit of textbooks or formal lessons—so most children, with help from those around them who are literate, develop the ability to read. The power of reading is a mystery, but for most people it is an available mystery, like the rising of the sun each day or the freshness of the rain.

Reading is part of a child's total language development—listening, speaking, writing, reading. It builds naturally on the language capacity that the child already has. By the time the typical child enters first grade, he has a speaking vocabulary of about 4,000 words. He has seen printed words and letters all around him—on cereal boxes, on television, on street signs, in magazines and newspapers—and he has watched adults read these words, speak them, make sense of them. He has a natural drive to explore and master this print environment as well. Gradually he comes to recognize a basic core of words on sight, words like *the, and, is, of, stop,* and perhaps *TV* and *Jeff* (his name). This core expands rapidly as formal instruction continues, always building on the child's speaking vocabulary. Meanwhile, the child learns to associate individual letters and combinations of letters with sounds and to *blend* these sounds into whole words. He learns to use the context of a passage or other clues, such as pictures, to help determine the sound and meaning of a word, as in the example "The _____ ran away." He moves gradually from known words to unknown words, and through speaking, listening, and reading he enlarges both his speaking and his reading vocabulary. Always he tries to get the meaning of a passage as well as to recognize the words, relating what he reads to his own experience. Eventually he learns to interpret what he reads—to describe the main idea, to locate key details, to identify cause/effect relationships, to make inferences.

The developmental process of learning to read has been likened to a journey. There is no single step that enables a person to read. Rather, there are many related steps that must be put together before one gets anywhere. Nor is there a single, set route or sequence that must be followed. There are many ways to get from here to there; what counts is the quality of the trip and what progress one makes. It is not even clear that one arrives at a final destination—that of being a fluent, accomplished reader—because reading, like playing the violin or hitting baseballs, is something that is never fully mastered. It is a skill to be developed through a lifetime of practice.

Nevertheless, the early steps of this journey are of great importance. You want you child to begin securely, to make sure progress, to enjoy his learning experience, and to feel confident of his developing ability. How do teachers help children take these steps, and what can you as a parent do to help?

HOW DO TEACHERS TEACH CHILDREN TO READ?

When Should Your Child Begin?

Most children can benefit from instruction in oral and printed language in kindergarten and even preschool. Almost all children are ready for appropriate instruction in first grade.

This contemporary view, amply supported by research, runs counter to the older view of readiness. For decades in this country the prevalent belief was that children should not begin formal reading instruction until they were sufficiently mature, usually at about the age of six and a half. To begin earlier, it was thought, would frustrate the child and have harmful consequences. Until children attained this maturity, they were made to concentrate upon the skills of readiness: naming colors, identifying shapes, using scissors, mastering certain physical skills, like hopping and skipping. When our youngest child was in first grade, we were told that he was not ready to be assigned to a reading group because he lacked "small muscle coordination." Upon inquiry, we learned that that meant that he could not tie his shoes. We knew why he couldn't tie his shoes: he was the baby of the family, and we had never taught him. We suggested that we would teach him to tie his shoes and the teacher should teach him to read. We did, she did, and all has gone well since.

There was a germ of truth to this idea of readiness. Children should not be made to try to do what they are simply incapable of doing. Some children are not developmentally ready to begin formal reading instruction at the beginning of first grade. Nor is there any overwhelming advantage to learning to read a few months earlier rather than later. Accordingly, children should not be subject to undue pressure to begin reading.

What we now know, however, is that all children, regardless of their stage of development, profit from appropriate experience with language—first listening and speaking, then writing and reading. The richer the child's language environment, the better. The earlier this richness, the better. The task of the first-grade teacher, like that of the kindergarten teacher before her, is to provide a rich program of language instruction appropriate to the child's developmental state. As a practical matter in today's society, this usually means a formal program of instruction in how to read.

Word Recognition Skills

In order to read well, a child must develop word recognition skills and comprehension skills. Good teachers teach them simultaneously.

Word recognition skills consist of *sight word* skills and *word attack* skills. Sight word skills enable a reader to recognize a word instantly on sight, as the reader of this passage no doubt is doing. Word attack skills enable readers to *decode* a passage—to pronounce the unfamiliar printed words and gain meaning from the page. Among the word attack skills are configuration clues, picture clues, context clues, phonic analysis, and structural analysis. We'll see what these mean in the following pages.

Sight Word Skills

By first grade many children have acquired a basic core of words that they recognize on sight—perhaps their name and some common words, such as *a, cat,* and *and.* No matter what method is used to teach reading, this sight vocabulary is useful in helping children learn other skills. Which sentence would it be easier for you to "read":

Y zink garped zed froom.

or

A cat garped the froom.

The familiar words help to map a territory in which word attack skills can be developed and employed effectively. Teachers help children acquire a useful fund of sight words through repeated practice. The sight vocabulary of beginning readers increases rapidly with practice in reading.

Word Attack Skills

CONFIGURATION CLUES

The beginning reader may use the shape of a word to help in identifying a word's pronunciation and meaning. For example, he may identify the word *pony* because the printed word has a tail like a real pony; he may identify the word *bee* because it is the only word he knows with two *e*'s. Obviously, these clues do not take a reader very far, and they tend to drop quickly from use as the child progresses.

PICTURE CLUES

The beginning reader is often also given picture clues to help identify unfamiliar words. The child who cannot otherwise say or attach meaning to the word *elephant* can do so when the page contains a picture of an elephant. (The word *elephant* may then become a known sight word because of its configuration.) Such pictures are widely used in beginning reading books. Like configuration clues, however, picture clues rapidly become less useful as the printed words become more abstract and as fewer pictures are provided. Such clues are like training wheels on a bicycle— perhaps a useful way to get started, but nothing to depend upon for a lifetime.

CONTEXT CLUES

Often a reader may be able to identify an unknown word by its placement among known words. For example, the child may not otherwise know the word *hungry* but can identify it correctly in the sentence, "The hungry monkey ate six bananas." Even experienced readers use such context clues, as you might in this sentence: "Because this is a book to teach parents about teaching, its style is often *didactic.*" Again, the placement of the relatively unknown word among known words helps the reader to give it proper meaning. Capable readers combine sight vocabulary and context skills throughout their reading lifetime.

PHONICS

Perhaps the beginning reading skill most familiar to the layman is phonic analysis. Phonics involves the relationship of letters to sounds. Children are taught to identify letters and groups of letters, to associate an appropriate sound with each letter or letter group, and to blend the separate sounds together so as to pronounce the word. Once the child has grasped the principle of letter-sound relationships and a fund of appropriate letter sounds, he has a key that enables him to decode a limitless number of unfamiliar printed words.

Phonics programs vary in their scope, design, and thoroughness. Almost all, however, begin by teaching the sounds of initial consonants (*c*at, *d*og, *m*an, and so on) and proceed in one order or another with the following:

- Consonants occurring in the word (bo*x*, bu*tt*er).
- Consonants that have two sounds (*c*ar, *c*ity).
- Consonant clusters and digraphs (*str*ing, *ch*air).
- Short and long vowel sounds (c*a*t, g*a*te).
- Vowel diphthongs and digraphs (b*oy*, m*ea*t).
- Silent letters (*k*nit, lam*b*).

When the skills of phonetic analysis are taught well— thoroughly, but as an aid to understanding not as an end in themselves—they are a powerful reading tool and, incidentally, an aid to correct spelling. How surprising, then, that phonics has been the subject of so much controversy in American education in recent decades! For most of our history, beginning readers were taught the letters of the alphabet, the sounds with which they were associated, and the skill of blending the sounds together to make words. In the 1920s many educators rebelled against this traditional approach and introduced the *look-say*, or *whole word*, method of teaching reading. Instead of constructing words from individual sounds, children were taught to recognize the whole word, as adult readers do. In the 1950s writers such as Rudolf Flesch (*Why Johnny Can't Read*) attacked the look-say method, blaming it for whatever reading deficiencies then existed. The controversy continued for years afterward.

By now, however, the controversy has become a red herring. Virtually no one believes that phonics should not be taught. Although some groups, like the Council for Basic Education in Washington, D.C., and the Reading Reform Foundation in Scottsdale, AZ, continue to call for an increased emphasis on phonics, few believe that phonics should be taught exclusively. The questions are, how much phonics should be taught, when, and in what manner? In the authors' view, the most sensible advice has been given by the report of the Commission on Reading: "The right maxims for phonics are: Do it early. Keep it simple. Except in cases of diagnosed individual need, phonics instruction should have been completed by the end of the second grade."

STRUCTURAL ANALYSIS

Beginning readers are taught to identify unknown words by dividing them into syllables, pronouncing each syllable, and blending the sounds of the parts to get the whole. In time, they are also taught to separate root words from prefixes and suffixes and to recognize common endings, such as -ed, -ing, -er, and -est. This structural analysis is a useful addition to the child's repertoire of word attack skills.

Comprehension Skills

Without an effective set of word recognition skills, no child can read. Obviously, it is of the utmost importance that such skills be taught thoroughly and mastered early in the process of learning to read.

At the same time, reading well is more than the ability to pronounce unfamiliar words and attach meaning to them in isolation. It involves comprehending the sense of the entire passage, following the story, understanding the point, noting the telling detail, bringing to bear one's own imagination and thinking, and so on. Recent studies suggest that American schoolchildren are weaker in these skills of reading comprehension than children in some other countries. For this reason, as well as to help children make sense of their classroom experience, most good contemporary reading programs stress both comprehension skills and word recognition skills from the very beginning.

Comprehension skills enable a child to understand the meaning of a passage, to make use of the information it contains, and to apply it appropriately to other situations. They include such skills as identifying the main idea of a paragraph or a passage, locating important details, recognizing cause/effect relationships, predicting outcomes, making inferences, and solving problems. At the first-grade level, these skills are almost always taught through discussion with the child about something he has read, as illustrated by the following scene from a first-grade classroom:

Early June. The children have read a story about animals. The teacher says, "Let's think about the story. What's the main thing that's happening? What's the most important thing?"

A child answers. "The animals need a home."

"Is that right?" the teacher asks the others in the group.

"Yes," they say.

"What else is important? Don't tell me the whole story. John said the chicken and the duck need a home. What else is important? What do you remember?"

The children respond. Later she asks, "Do you think it would be a good home for the bear?"

"No," says a child. "It's too small."

"Just like Jelly," says the teacher. "Do you remember when Jelly [the guinea pig] was trying to get into her home because she was so scared, but she could only get her head in because she was so pregnant?" The teacher consistently helps the children relate the story to their experience. At the end of the discussion she asks, "Do you think the story is sad, happy, or funny? It could be a combination, too."

Reading for these children and this teacher is more than developing and applying a set of skills. It is understanding a passage, thinking about it, enjoying discussing it, relating it to experience. This kind of attention to the content of a passage, which involves the development of comprehension skills, should proceed hand in hand with the development of word recognition skills. And if the child is helped to *enjoy* his reading experience, the likelihood that he will want to continue to read is of course increased.

BASAL READERS

Basal reading programs are used by about 90 percent of America's primary-school (grades K–2) teachers and about 75 percent of its intermediate (grades 3–6) teachers. These programs (and the relatively few publishing companies that produce and market them) exert a strong influence on the way America's children are taught to read.

Basal reading programs are complete packages of materials for teaching reading. They can be used alone, as the entire reading curriculum, or in combination with other teaching approaches. (We shall describe some of these other approaches later in this chapter.) Typically, they consist of a *scope and sequence* chart, which lists in order the skills to be learned; a graded set of books, or *readers*, for children to read; sets of practice exercises for children, in the form of workbooks and worksheets; teacher's manuals, which describe in great detail the steps the teacher is to follow; and a variety of supplemental materials, such as tests, charts, word cards, sentence cards, audiotapes, filmstrips, and supplementary reading books. A complete basal reading program for grades K–6 would fill at least two large cardboard boxes.

The programs organize their materials into reading levels that roughly correspond to the grade structure of American schools. A typical arrangement is as follows:

Level 1—Readiness
Level 2—Preprimer
Level 3—Primer
Level 4—First reader
Level 5—First half of second grade
Level 6—Second half of second grade
Level 7—First half of third grade
Level 8—Second half of third grade
Level 9—Fourth grade

Level 10—Fifth grade
Level 11—Sixth grade

The programs follow certain basic principles. They arrange their reading materials in a progression of gradually increasing difficulty, teaching all the reading skills in sequential fashion. The vocabulary used in the readers is limited to words that are thought to be within the children's listening and speaking vocabularies. (Surprisingly, the lists of words vary substantially from publisher to publisher. However, a total of about 500 words is typically introduced by the end of the first reader.) The number of new words in each reading selection is carefully controlled, and familiar words are repeated for reinforcement. The number of words in each sentence is kept small. Most of the selections are in story form and are based on experiences supposedly familiar to the child. (Traditionally, the standard story was about a middle-class suburban family in which there is a father who goes to work, a mother who keeps house, two children who never fight, and a variety of pets who jump and run. In recent years, some series have introduced characters who live in cities in different family circumstances. However, much of the middle-class stereotype remains in the readers used in many American classrooms.) Finally, the basal programs are designed to be a total reading program, complete in themselves. And for many teachers, particularly beginning teachers or those without access to other resources, they do constitute most or all of the reading program in the primary grades.

The typical basal reader lesson consists of five steps:

1. The teacher prepares the children by motivating them to read the story, by discussing new words that appear in the story, by reminding them of skills already learned (such as certain phonic skills or the use of particular punctuation marks), by discussing concepts on which the story may be based (in the story "The Magic Hats" referred to below, the concept of imagination).

2. The children are given a purpose for reading and asked to read the story silently.
3. The children read all or part of the story aloud and discuss it with the teacher.
4. The teacher assigns follow-up activities according to children's individual needs. (Some may practice a skill just taught in the lesson; others may practice an old skill; still others may apply the new skill on a more sophisticated level.)
5. The teacher introduces a variety of activities to reinforce and expand the skill just taught. Children may read another story on a related theme, or they may draw a picture or write stories of their own.

Obviously, these steps can be combined or emphasized differently, but most basal lessons follow a somewhat similar pattern.

In the Harcourt Brace Jovanovich series, for example, the level 4 (first reader) book *Sun and Shadow* contains a story, "The Magic Hats," about a girl who on a rainy day puts on a variety of hats and imagines herself to be the person who would wear such a hat. Complete with pictures, the story is only five pages long; the suggested treatment of this story in the accompanying teacher's guide runs to eleven full pages, devoted to the steps "Preparing to Read," "Reading and Discussing," "Maintaining Skills," "Providing for Individual Differences," and "Enrichment."

INDIVIDUALIZED READING PROGRAMS

An alternative to the basal reading program in teaching children to read is the individualized reading program. In such a program the books that the child reads are selected by the child himself with guidance by the teacher. The child chooses books that interest him and that are of an appropriate level of reading difficulty. The teacher, meanwhile, ensures that the selected books are at the right level of skills development, monitors the child's progress through frequent individual conferences, and develops appropriate independent study activities for the child.

Such a program, while it may seem to be directed by the child's interests (indeed, the child may actually experience it that way), in fact requires much knowledge and planning on the part of the teacher. The teacher must determine each child's reading skills needs so that she can help children choose books appropriate for their instructional level. She must come to know and remember each child's reading interests. She must know in what kind of setting and with what kind of material each child works best. She must know and make available a wide range of books and instructional materials. She must make time for frequent individual conferences. And she must keep full and careful records of each child's experience and progress.

The advantages of an individualized program are that each child is reading books at his own level of difficulty; he is not held back or pulled ahead by other children in the group; and he learns skills as he needs them. Because the child chooses the books, his level of motivation is presumably higher, and because the potential range of reading material is broader than in a basal series, there are more opportunities to read books of literary worth.

Because of the difficulty of teaching such a program, as well as from a concern that all children experience the same lessons so as to avoid "gaps" in their instruction, relatively few classroom teachers organize their reading programs in this manner. (More typically, one sees teachers using an individualized approach with the top readers involved in a basal program.) In the authors' view, the parent whose child is involved in an individualized program, provided that it is taught by an experienced and energetic teacher, is truly lucky. If your child is involved in a basal program, you may wish to raise some of the questions suggested later in this chapter.

LANGUAGE-EXPERIENCE PROGRAMS

The language-experience approach to the teaching of reading emphasizes the unity of all language activity—listening, speaking, writing, reading. Individually or in groups, the child writes or dictates stories out of his experience. He reads what he has written or what others have written for him. The teacher helps the child to build upon these experiences—enriching them with other reading material and with appropriate instructional activities—to achieve increasing levels of reading proficiency and language facility. The core of a language-experience program consists of the stories or pieces written by the child himself. Ideally, the child learns to read whatever he can say, and since children's speaking vocabulary is much larger than the vocabulary of the typical basal reading series, a rich store of language is available. Children write about classroom activities, field trips, stories and poems, films, videotapes, their families, holidays—whatever they are interested in and whatever the teacher interests them in. The teacher helps the child write what he can say but cannot yet write himself. Speaking, writing, and reading about these topics serve as a means of communicating with another person. The teacher pays foremost attention to the content of the child's writing and reading, providing a ready and respectful audience. The presence of a real audience is very important. Often the child's stories are collected and made into a "book" to be read by other children in the class and by adults.

Although children develop skills of reading and writing through this process, direct instruction about skills is also pursued separately. The teacher must maintain careful records and occasionally teach children skills they need. One commonly used device is a *word bank*. The child keeps a collection of the words he has used in his stories, each written on a separate card. These word cards can then be used in teaching phonics (put all words that begin with *p* together), structural analysis (all words with three syllables), alphabetization (first letter; first two letters), vocabulary development (all synonyms together), and so on. Whatever device is used, this sort of supplementary skills instruction is important.

The advantage of the language-experience approach is its direct relevance to the interests and abilities of the child. However, the lack of an orderly progression of skills development imposes a great burden on the teacher to keep records and to provide needed learning opportunities. In addition, the child eventually outgrows his speaking vocabulary. For these reasons, this approach is most commonly used where it can be most effective— with beginning readers or, in later grades, with those children who are reading below grade level.

DIAGNOSTIC/PRESCRIPTIVE TEACHING

Whatever kind of reading program your first-grade child is involved in—a basal reading program, an individualized program, a language-experience program, or some combined approach— the effective teacher is likely to supplement her work with a diagnostic/prescriptive approach to skills development. No matter how systematic the reading program, children will vary in their general levels of mastery and in the order in which they acquire specific skills. Accordingly, the teacher will employ a variety of means to diagnose an individual child's specific reading skills needs and prescribe activities to help him meet them.

A diagnostic/prescriptive approach involves at least five steps:

1. The teacher determines the skills to be acquired and the order in which they are to be taught. Sometimes teachers follow the scope and sequence of skills provided by the publisher of the basal reading series they are using. Sometimes they develop their own skills charts, based on their experiences and their knowledge of the class. Sometimes schools or school systems

develop charts for use by all teachers, in order to promote continuity from grade to grade. There is no one best way to order the skills required in learning to read. What is important is that there be a plan and that the teacher know how your child stands in relation to it.

2. The teacher determines which skills the child has already mastered and has yet to master at his instructional level. This diagnosis may be made by giving a formal test, or it may be made informally through observing or conferencing with the child. Some teachers use diagnostic tests from commercial publishing houses. (More about these tests in the chapter "Tests in the Primary Years," p. 234) Some make up tests from the workbook pages or exercises in basal reading series teacher's manuals. Depending on the nature of the test and of the child, the test may be given individually or in a small or large group.

3. The teacher provides instruction in the skill to be developed. Usually she conducts a direct lesson in which she introduces and demonstrates the skill, then provides, or *prescribes*, activities for the child so he can practice and reinforce what he has been taught. These activities may be of many forms, for example, worksheets, games, puzzles, writing, or projects with other children. Since children do not all learn in the same way, good teachers provide many and varied opportunities for children to learn.

4. The teacher determines whether or not the child has learned the needed skill. The procedures are generally the same as those used for making a diagnosis, although the specific material or activities may vary. Teachers often test for *mastery* of a skill immediately after the child has finished the learning activity. Good teachers also test again some time later, to be sure that a skill has been thoroughly mastered.

5. The teacher provides for appropriate follow-up activity. Within the diagnostic/prescriptive sequence, this may mean diagnosis of a new skill, or it may mean additional practice to reinforce recently acquired skills.

Again, this systematic attention to the specific skills needs of individual children is an important component of any effective reading program.

READING FOR FUN

As critically important as the skills of reading surely are, they alone will not guarantee that your child will become a true reader—one who likes to read, who reads for information and for pleasure, whose life is enriched by reading. Such attitudes and habits are formed early. Good first-grade teachers know as much. They provide an environment that encourages reading and a rich array of reading activities above and beyond those devoted to the development of skills.

The means by which teachers encourage even beginning readers to read are many. Some classrooms have reading corners, where an old easy chair or a rug or a shelf of attractive books invites quiet reading. Many have bright new book jackets tacked to the wall and children's stories about books attractively displayed. Some classes create large murals depicting stories they have read, or act out plays. Some have book fairs at which children can sample a wide array of library books or inexpensive paperbacks. And always, in good reading classes, the teacher will read aloud to the class, sharing her enthusiasm for the story and her love of reading in general, and will also provide ample time for the children to read quietly by themselves.

The school library or town library can be a valuable asset to a recreational reading program. If possible, however, each classroom should have its own small library as well. In the authors' experience, the test is very simple: in classrooms that contain many books, children are likely to be reading. In classrooms that do not, the likelihood is less.

HOW DO TEACHERS ORGANIZE A CLASS FOR READING INSTRUCTION?

So far we have discussed how children are taught to read without emphasizing the group nature of the experience. The fact is, however, that most children do not receive reading instruction from an individual tutor. Much more likely, they are part of a group of twenty-odd children, all in different states of learning readiness, skills development ability, and background. By the time the class is in the middle of the first-grade year, a range in reading achievement of four levels or more is not unusual.

How do teachers cope with these numbers and this diversity? How does a teacher teach so many different children to read, in a manner that is appropriate for each?

Grouping

In the first grade almost all reading instruction occurs individually or in small groups. Few lessons are taught to the whole class at one time. Consequently, the teacher must plan how to divide the class, and she must provide for those children with whom she is not working at the moment. The teacher divides the class into three or more groups of five to nine pupils each. While she works directly with one group, the others are assigned seatwork or other tasks related to the reading program.

In the classic arrangement, children used to be divided into groups according to their reading level and ability. Many of us remember or have heard about the "Bluebirds," the "Robins," and the "Crows." In this way, children presumably received instruction appropriate to their level. But there were problems. The Crows quickly came to know who they were; they internalized a poor image of themselves and tended to fulfill the prophecy that they would not do well. The Robins never heard the Bluebirds (or the Crows) read, and an aspiring Robin rarely had the chance to change the color of his feathers and become a Bluebird. The Bluebirds lacked interaction with other children who had much to give, and occasionally they became a bit stuck on themselves.

Effective teachers now vary the composition of their groups according to achievement level, interests, and specific skills needs. The basis for grouping may change from day to day or even within a single reading period, and the groups themselves change from time to time. In this way all the children interact with one another, avoiding the stigma of being less able while still functioning at a level appropriate to their ability.

For example, the teacher may divide the class into three groups according to reading level: Bill's group, Max's group, and Maria's group. She may also organize the whole class into four interest groups: Jill's, Paula's, Harry's, and Tom's. During the reading period on a given day, she may have the class meet by reading-level groups for the first two twenty-minute segments and by interest groups for the third twenty-minute segment. On that day her program looks like this:

9:10–9:30	Bill's group (Teacher hears them read)	Max's group (Seatwork)	Maria's group (Seatwork)
9:30–9:50	Bill's group (Seatwork)	Max's group (Teacher introduces new skill)	Maria's group (Seatwork)
9:50–10:10	Jill's group, Paula's group, and Harry's group (Work on projects)		Tom's group (Teacher helps with project)

On another day, the teacher may organize small groups according to specific skills needs. On that day her reading period program may look like this:

9:10–9:40	Bill's group (Seatwork)	Max's group (Seatwork)	Maria's group (Teacher hears them read)
9:40–9:55	John's group (Teacher reviews and reinforces a previously taught skill)	Rest of class (Seatwork)	
19:55–10:10	Sally's group (Teacher introduces new skill)	Rest of class (Seatwork)	

While working directly with a group, the teacher may be diagnosing needs, assessing interests, motivating an activity, listening to children read, discussing what the children have read, teaching a new skill or reinforcing one previously taught, or conducting a wide range of similar activities, often more than one simultaneously.

Meanwhile, the other children are working individually or in small groups at what is conventionally known as *seatwork*. In too many classrooms, such activity consists largely of filling out commercially prepared worksheets keyed to the lesson just taught. ("Circle the objects that begin with the *m* sound.") Such exercises have some usefulness, but they do not begin to mine the riches of the language available. In well-run classes, children also spend time doing the following:

- Writing—starting a new piece, revising an old one.
- Reading—the story the teacher just assigned, something from the library corner.
- Playing word games—some tied to specific skills, some for vocabulary building.
- Researching newspapers and magazines—perhaps on a topic related to an interest group (even looking for pictures).

- Making a picture of something they have read.
- Illustrating their own storybooks.
- Printing a newsletter.
- Listening to a story on an audiocassette.

The variety of interesting and instructive activities is virtually limitless. The teacher's task is to keep the activity imaginative, alive, and as full of different learning opportunities as possible. The child should always be so fully and appropriately engaged that neither he nor the teacher ever comes to regard this time and activity as busywork.

Individual Differences

By organizing small groups within the class and providing each child with learning opportunities suited to his reading level, developmental level, interests, and skills needs, teachers do much to attend to the individual differences among pupils in a class. Some teachers feel that provision should also be made for the child's individual learning style.

Research has not as yet elucidated why one child learns best under one set of conditions and another child under another set; nor has it allowed us to understand fully the reasons for existing differences. Some children (and adults) learn best visually; some through hearing. Some process information mentally; some need to handle objects or at least to write things down. Some (presumably those whose left brain is dominant) proceed in sequential fashion from step 1 to step 2 to step 3; some (presumably those whose right brain is dominant) prefer to jump into the middle of things and explore the terrain before sorting things out. For example, in learning word processing, one of the authors preferred to follow the manual step by step, while the other began by plunging directly into the program, referring to the manual only when help was needed.) Some require a relaxed, supportive environment when learning something new; some profit from an atmosphere lightly charged with tension. Some work best alone, some with one other person, some in small or large groups.

The role of the teacher is not so much to ascertain each child's style of learning as to provide many different ways of learning the necessary material. A child working on a phonics skill might work with written word games (sight), listen to audiotapes (hearing), and place the letter blocks in the appropriate pile (touch). He might work alone for a while, then in a small group. When the teacher sees how he makes the most rapid progress, she can give him more of that kind of work to do.

One of our children was slow to read. In January, his first-grade teacher, an experienced and effective woman, gave him a primer from a series heavily based on phonics. For the first time the letters and words began to make sense to him; before long, he was reading. When we asked how she knew that these materials would be appropriate for him, she said, "I just had a hunch." Her theoretical knowledge might not have impressed a professor of psychology, but her practical skill in providing alternate learning materials taught our child to read.

Much depends upon the informed intuition of sensible teachers such as these. In the end, what counts is not how well the teacher can explain what she is doing, but how well she is helping your child to learn and grow.

WHAT TO LOOK FOR IN A GOOD FIRST-GRADE READING PROGRAM

Reading programs that follow the good principles and practices described above are likely to be effective for your child. Unfortunately, not all teaching is equally effective, and you will probably not be able to follow the day-to-day course of reading instruction in your child's classroom. However, as we said about the kindergarten, every parent can tell whether certain key qualities of a good first-grade reading program are present or absent. If the answers to most or all of the following questions are yes, chances are your child is participating in an effective program. If many of the answers are no, you may want to inquire further by talking with your child's teacher and, possibly, the principal.

What to Look for in the Classroom

When you visit your child's classroom, do you see

- An environment that encourages reading, with displays of stories, book jackets, posters, printed signs naming the objects to which they are attached, displays of stories children have written or dictated, pictures children have made about stories they have read?
- Many books for recreational reading, placed where children may get them easily?
- A quiet corner or spot for silent reading?
- Many materials for use in reading instruction, including magazines, catalogs, games, puzzles, plastic or magnetic letters, filmstrips, and audiotapes, as well as worksheets?

What to Look for From Your Child

Does your child

- Show interest and enthusiasm for learning to read?
- Try to read simple words in his environment, such as traffic signs, bus signs, easy words on packaged goods or in television commercials, words in stories you read to him?
- Talk about reading he has done in school?
- Bring home stories or pictures about reading he has done in school?
- Bring home worksheets, games, puzzles, or other material that shows evidence of skills instruction?

- Demonstrate that he has grasped the connection between letters and sounds?
- Understand the stories you read and discuss together?

What to Look for From the Teacher

When you talk to your child's teacher, does she

- Know your child's reading level, interests, and attitudes toward reading?
- Describe specifically the progress your child is making?
- Describe her overall approach to teaching reading?
- Show you many different kinds of books and other materials that she uses to teach word recognition and comprehension skills?
- Describe the stories, poems, and activities that are part of the children's recreational reading program?

HOW TO HELP YOUR CHILD AT HOME

Now that your child has become a first grader, the primary responsibility for his formal instruction has shifted from you to his teacher. However, there are things that you can do at home to support the work your child and his teacher are doing at school.

Do's

- Praise and encourage your child's successful efforts to read.
- Continue to read to your child often, every day if possible. You may wish to set aside a certain time each day—at bedtime or

after dinner—when you and your child get together for your own special reading time.

- Encourage your child to read to you *when he feels comfortable doing so.*
- Pronounce for your child the words he cannot pronounce himself when he is reading to you. Don't expect him to know all the words in the language or to display mastery of phonics skills. Let your reading together be fun; don't make it into a test.
- Buy your child books as presents; make them special.
- Visit the library with your child and help him choose books that he may like.
- Limit the amount of television your child is allowed to watch. Research shows that viewing television for about ten hours per week may actually aid reading achievement. Beyond this amount, achievement tends to decline.
- Make constructive use of the television your child does watch. Be selective about the programs he sees; talk with him about the content of the programs; find reading material related to matters that interest him on television.
- Talk often with your child to help him enlarge his vocabulary and to use language to think and to express himself.
- Confer periodically with your child's teacher to learn about his progress at school.

Don'ts

- Don't pressure your child into reading if he seems reluctant or uncomfortable.
- Don't make the child demonstrate what he is learning. For example, don't ask him to sound out words with which he is having trouble. Again, reading with you should be a pleasure, not a test.
- Don't try to do the teacher's job. Leave formal instruction to

her. Otherwise, you may end up frustrating or confusing your child.

- Don't criticize the teacher in front of your child. You will destroy the confidence he needs to do well. Save your comments for the teacher herself or the principal.

THE SIGNS OF PROGRESS

Children differ in their rates of growth. Physically, emotionally, and mentally, some children develop sooner than others. For this reason it is not uncommon to find that by the end of the first-grade year some children are reading at the third- or fourth-grade level while others have not yet learned to read.

Remember that rates of development are not necessarily related to intelligence, any more than the early flowers of spring are necessarily more beautiful or sturdier than those that bloom late in the summer. If your child is reading well for his age by the end of first grade, be thankful and continue to encourage him. If he is not, you may wish to arrange for testing to determine whether his condition is the result of delayed development or some other problem (see the chapter "The Child With Learning Problems"). But in either case, remember that your child's progress should be measured in terms of his own developmental rate and not that of other children.

Word Recognition Skills

With the above ideas in mind, by the end of the first-grade year you should expect your child to

- Recognize, pronounce, and understand a sight vocabulary of about 200 simple words.

- Understand the principle of letter-sound correspondence, that is, that letters represent sounds.
- Pronounce the appropriate sounds of single consonants, the common consonant clusters (like *tr*, *pl*), vowels, and diphthongs when they appear in simple words.
- Blend known letter sounds into simple words.
- Use phonics skills and context clues to identify simple unknown words.

Comprehension Skills

Given reading material on the first-grade level, your child by the end of the year should be able to

- Understand the meaning of simple sentences from the order of the words.
- Find significant details within a sentence or a paragraph.
- Relate reading to illustrations.
- Understand the meaning of simple paragraphs.
- Recognize and understand negative sentences.
- Recognize time intervals.
- Recognize cause and effect.
- Predict outcomes based on what is known.

Attitudes

You should expect your child by the end of the first year to

- Enjoy having stories and poems read aloud.
- Enjoy reading simple stories and poems.
- Feel positive about progress made in school.

Mathematics in the First Grade

School days, school days
Good old Golden Rule days
Reading and writing and 'rithmetic
Taught to the tune of the hickory stick . . .

The hickory stick has all but disappeared, but the trinity of the three R's remains at the center of the school curriculum. As well it should. For if your child is to understand the highly technological world in which he will live, a solid grounding in mathematics is as necessary as the ability to read and write.

Unfortunately, during the past three decades there has been considerable confusion about just what mathematics should be taught in schools and how. When your child's grandparents were in elementary, or grammar, school, the mathematics curriculum was essentially arithmetic—addition, subtraction, multiplication, and division. The emphasis was upon fast and accurate computation; most teaching involved repeated drill and practice. About the time that Sputnik was launched in 1957, many teachers and scholars recognized the limitations of this approach. They created the new math, which included other forms of mathematics, such as geometry, statistics, probability, functions, and graphing, and which emphasized the development of thinking and understanding instead of learning by rote. In these respects the new math was a valuable educational advance.

Unfortunately, the new approach was excessively formalistic and preoccupied with the precise use of abstract language that often made little sense to children. For example, much time was spent trying to teach beginners the difference between a *number* and a *numeral*, an important distinction for the more sophisticated, but one at best confusing for a child just learning to count. For these reasons, and perhaps because children spent less time practicing computational skills, test scores declined and reaction inevitably followed. The back-to-basics movement of the 1970s featured a return to an emphasis on computation and to a teaching style characterized by drill and practice.

Today, good schools and good teachers have learned to follow a sensible middle course. They know that a curriculum consisting of addition, subtraction, multiplication, and division alone is not enough. They also know that in an age of readily available calculators and computers, a preoccupation with the skills of computation is unwise. Children should still learn their number facts, but they should spend much more of their time developing an ability to solve problems through the use of mathematics. The excesses of the old new math can be avoided as teachers help children develop their ability to think. As we said in the chapter "Mathematics in the Kindergarten," what is important is that children learn to use the power of mathematical thinking to bring greater clarity or order to their experience. Mathematics is not just a set of facts and procedures—it is an activity of the mind.

THE FIRST-GRADE MATHEMATICS CURRICULUM

Most first-grade mathematics curricula comprise five parts, or *strands*, as they are sometimes called:

Numbers and numeration
Operations with whole numbers
Operations with fractions
Probability and statistics
Geometry and measurement

Some schools include a sixth part, problem solving. In the authors' view, however, problem solving is the goal of all mathematics and should be incorporated into the teaching and learning of each part of the curriculum.

The sequence in which the curriculum is taught and the emphasis placed on each part vary from school to school. But throughout the United States, first-grade mathematics programs are much more similar than they are different from one another.

The five main parts of the mathematics curriculum are taught throughout the elementary grades. In the first grade, the skills and knowledge that children should acquire are as follows.

Numbers and Numeration

- Sorting and classifying: Continue to develop number concepts through sorting and classifying concrete objects.
- Sets: Compare sets of objects with more, less, and the same amounts. Match number words and symbols with sets of objects from zero to twenty.
- Counting—cardinal numbers: Learn to use cardinal numbers to twenty-first (or beyond) with sets of objects and a number line.
- One-to-many correspondence: Understand that a single object may represent a group of many objects. *Example:* a dime represents ten pennies. Use coins, blocks or rods appropriately to reflect this understanding.
- Numerals: Develop the ability to read and write numerals from at least 0 to 100. Understand the meaning of each digit in two-digit numbers: *Example:* 27 = 2 tens and 7 ones. Recognize

fraction numerals with a numerator of 1 and a denominator of 1–9. Recognize money notation to $9.99.

Operations With Whole Numbers

• Grouping: Group concrete objects by twos, threes, fives, tens. Understand concept of even and odd numbers.
• Renaming: Understand that a number has many names: *Example:*

$$\begin{array}{llll} 4 & 1+3 & 1+1+1+1 \\ \text{four} & 2+2 & 5-1 \\ \text{quatre} & 1+1+2 & 8-4 \end{array}$$

• Addition and subtraction: Learn addition and subtraction facts through 10. Learn role of zero in addition and subtraction. Understand that the order of numbers to be added does not change the sum. *Example:* 4 + 3 = 7; 3 + 4 = 7. (This principle is called the commutative law.) Learn to add three numbers that sum to 10 or less: *Example*   2 + 1 + 2 = 5. Understand that addition and subtraction are opposite operations: *Example*   3 + 4 = 7; 7 − 4 = 3; 7 − 3 = 4.
• Place value: Add and subtract two two-digit numbers that do not require regrouping (carrying), using base 10 materials: *Example:*

$$\begin{array}{lll} 33 & 3 \text{ tens} & 3 \text{ ones} \\ \underline{+21} & \underline{+\ 2 \text{ tens}} & \underline{1 \text{ one}} \\ & 5 \text{ tens} & 4 \text{ ones} \end{array}$$

• Operation symbols: Read and write number sentences using the symbols +, −, and = both vertically and horizontally: *Example:*

$$
\begin{array}{r}
2 \\
+3 \\
\hline
5
\end{array}
$$

Read and write number sentences using symbols > (is greater than) and < (is less than). Recognize symbol (   ) and complete open-number sentences: *Examples:* 4 + 3 = (   ); 7 − 4 = (   ); 4 + 3 < (   ); 7 − 4 > (   ).

- Patterns: Explore pattern for sums and differences in concrete materials and in number tables: *Examples*

6			±	1	2	3	4	5
0	6		1	2	3	4	5	6
1	5		2	3	4	5	6	7
2	4		3	4	5	6	7	8
3	3		4	5	6	7	8	9
			5	6	7	8	9	10

Operations With Fractions

- Equal parts of a whole: Divide a whole object into equal parts (halves, thirds, fourths, fifths). Divide a set of objects into equal parts (halves, thirds, fourths, fifths).
- Unequal parts of a whole: Understand that fractions may be unequal.
- Numerals: Read and write fractions with a numerator of 1 and a denominator of 1–9.

Probability and Statistics

- Data gathering and graphing: Collect, organize, and record information using two or more categories at a time: *Examples:* (1) Pile blocks to represent the number of children who prefer dogs and the number who prefer cats. (2) Make a chart showing the favorite colors of each child in the class.

- Tallying: Tally the information obtained by data gathering and graphing. Compare the amounts in each category: *Examples:* (1) More children like dogs than cats. (2) Six more children like red than the number liking yellow.
- Anticipating outcomes: Estimate the likelihood of events happening; compare estimate with actual outcome. Estimate the number of possible combinations within an arrangement; compare estimates with actual results: *Example:* How many pairs of numbers have a sum of 8?

Geometry and Measurement

- Estimating and making rough measurements: Continue concrete activities involving comparison of size, distance, weight, capacity, temperature, time. Make estimating an integral part of all measurement activity.
- Standard units of measure: Understand the need for standard units of measure. Measure lengths of objects in centimeters and inches. Use clocks and calendars to measure time in hours, days, months, years. Weigh objects in pounds and kilograms. Measure capacity in quarts, pints, and liters.
- Shapes: Continue to explore properties of two-dimensional shapes in the environment. Create geometric patterns and designs using blocks, counters, buttons, ink blots. Explore three-dimensional shapes in the classroom and in the environment, including cubes, prisms, spheres, cylinders, pyramids.

TEACHING THE FIRST-GRADE MATHEMATICS CURRICULUM

In kindergarten, much of the teaching and learning of mathematics was informal, a natural outgrowth of play activity or of classroom routines. Informal instruction occurs in the first grade as well, but teachers are also much more likely to schedule regular periods of time for mathematics instruction, to teach prepared lessons, and to schedule time for children to practice the skills and knowledge they are learning.

Like the good kindergarten classroom, the good first-grade classroom contains much evidence of mathematical activity. One sees number lines (on the wall above the blackboard or strung across the room), large calendars, clocks, a thermometer. There are blocks, rods, and chips for counting and sorting, and large jars of beans, marbles, or shells for estimating. Everywhere are graphs—of children's birthdays (month by month), of children's height, of the temperature (day by day), of teeth lost, of what was eaten for lunch (How many bologna sandwiches? How many peanut-butter sandwiches? How many cheese sandwiches?). There may be small slates or blackboards for easily erased practice work, and there may be an abacus (don't laugh: old-fashioned or not, a creative teacher can put the abacus to good use). Perhaps there are some pocket calculators, though these are rare at this level. And no doubt there are worksheets on the desks and on the walls, records of work the children have accomplished.

All this material is useful in mathematics instruction. But beyond that, seeing the material on display promotes a constant awareness of the way in which people think mathematically about the world around them. This awareness—that mathematics is not just for lessons but for life—is a primary objective of the first-grade program.

Teachers and schools vary in the ways they teach the mathematics curriculum. (In the authors' experience, there are often as many differences between one teacher and another within a school building as between one school district and another across the country.) Some teaching is formal, direct, didactic. The lessons are separate from the rest of the classroom experience: children know when they are studying mathematics and when they are moving on to something else. Other kinds of teaching may be less obviously controlled by the teacher. The math activity may grow more naturally out of a broader unit of study (like the study of the supermarket or of life in Colonial times) and be more connected to other activity in which the children are engaged. Parents should understand that there can be good teaching and poor teaching of both kinds. Either style can be effective, provided that teachers adhere to the few fundamental principles outlined below. Consider these examples of effective teaching:

An early morning in November. Right after class meeting, the teacher makes a large rectangle on the floor, using masking tape. She asks the children to pretend that it is a swimming pool. She has six children "jump" into the pool. (The children are delighted; they enjoy the physical activity and the memory of real swimming during the past summer.) She has two children climb out and stand nearby, then asks, "How many children are left in the pool?"

The class counts the children in the "pool" and says, "Four." The teacher writes "4" on the blackboard. The teacher asks the two children to jump back into the "pool" and has the others climb out.

She asks the class, "How many are left in the pool now?"

"Two," says one child, almost immediately. On the blackboard the teacher writes

$$
\begin{array}{cc}
6 & 6 \\
-2 & -4 \\
\hline
4 & 2
\end{array}
$$

The teacher asks, "How are these two facts the same? How are they different?"

The lesson continues, with different children "jumping" in and out of the "pool" in various combinations totaling six. Each time the children tell how many are left in the pool. The teacher writes all of the number facts on the blackboard, and the children discuss them with her. After several minutes the teacher asks the class to turn to a certain page in their workbooks and to fill in the boxes with the right answers to problems such as these:

$$
\begin{array}{cccc}
6 & 6 & 6 & 6 \\
-\,3 & -\,1 & \underline{} & \underline{} \\
\hline
& & 2 & 5
\end{array}
$$

January. The threat of snow outside, but a warm buzz within: in Updike's phrase, a sense of shelter. Nine children are elsewhere—some in the library, some with a special teacher for the gifted. A group of seventeen works with this teacher. For several days they have been working on a unit in nutrition; today each child has been asked to bring an apple. The teacher says, "Would someone please get the graphing cloth." A child goes immediately to a nearby cabinet and returns with a folded plastic tablecloth. He opens it and places it on the floor, the reverse side up. The teacher has marked it with masking tape to make boxes used in graphing—six columns, eight rows. The children sit around the cloth. The teacher asks them to place their apples on it.

"Who has an idea?" she asks.

A child says, "Colors." The children are familiar with this kind of activity, sorting objects by various properties.

A child says, "Red." The teacher writes the word *red* on a piece of posterboard and places it at the head of a column.

Another child says, "Yellow."

A third says, "Green." Each time the teacher writes the word and places it at the head of a column. A fourth child says, "Multi-color."

"Oh," says the teacher, "that's a new word for us. It's really two words, with a hyphen, or a dash, in between. What does it mean?"

The child says, "More than one color." The teacher writes *multi-color* on a piece of oaktag and places it at the head of a column.

A fifth child says, "Maroon."

Another child says, "Maroon is the same as red." Some children disagree. Rapid conversation ensues.

The teacher, taking charge, asks, "Do you think we have to take a vote?" All nod and say, "Yes." The teacher asks a child to get the ballots. (The class is familiar with this activity, too.) The ballots are blank pieces of oaktag; the child gives one to each pupil.

The teacher says, "We're going to see if 'maroon' should be another category. If you don't want 'maroon' to be a category, give me your ballots." Some children give her their ballots. "If you do want 'maroon' to be a category, give me your ballots." The rest of the children hand her their ballots.

"Let's count the ballots," she says. Together they count aloud six ballots against "maroon" and eleven ballots for "maroon." The teacher asks, "How many more votes are there for 'maroon' than against 'maroon'?"

A few children say, "Five."

She says, "Some people say, 'Five.' Let's see if they're right." The teacher places the ballots on the floor, matching each "no" vote with a "yes" vote until the "no" votes are matched. She asks the group to count the remaining five ballots.

Now the teacher prepares to write the word *maroon* on an oaktag. "Who can tell me how to spell *maroon?*" she asks. A child spells the word, and she writes it down. The categories are now complete. The teacher asks the group to place their apples in the boxes under the right color word. The children busy themselves with this activity, occasionally changing their minds about the appropriate category. When they have finished, she asks, "Who can tell us the results of the graph?"

One child points and says, "That's the most, and that's the least."

Another child says, "There are seven more multi-color than green."

The teacher says, "Let's count."

Another child says, "There are eight more multi-color than

maroon." They count again. The group continues to make comparisons of this kind, and to check them by counting.

After a few minutes the teacher says, "I have another idea about what to do with these apples." She takes out two paper plates and places four apples on one and two on another. She asks, "What do you see on the two plates?"

A child says, "One has four and one has two." (At this point two additional children return from the library; they join the group on the floor.)

The teacher asks, "How many all together?"

The group says, "Six." The teacher asks the group to get their small portable slates and chalk.

She says, "I'm going to write what I see on the plate. You write what you think you see." The teacher writes "4 + 2 = 6."

One girl has written

$$
\begin{array}{r}
4 \\
+\ 2 \\
\hline
6
\end{array}
$$

The teacher says, "Isn't that just as good? Doesn't that show the same thing?" The class agrees.

The teacher and class continue in this fashion, the teacher making different combinations of apples on the plates and the class writing different number facts on their slates. At one point a child writes "5" backward. The teacher says, "Don't worry. You can change it if it's going the wrong way."

Later, the teacher cuts open several of the apples and asks the children to count the seeds. They discover that all apples do not have the same number of seeds, and they talk about halves and quarters. Then they wash the apples and eat them for their morning snack.

Each of these lessons illustrates important principles of good mathematics teaching. Both begin with concrete objects—children in the "pool," apples on the cloth—and the teacher refers the class to them often to check accuracy and understanding. Both emphasize understanding as well as rote memory. Both involve activities that are pleasurable for the children and that make sense to them within their world. Both build on what children have learned before and both prepare the way for what will follow. Both allow ample time for practice.

WHAT TO LOOK FOR IN A GOOD FIRST-GRADE MATHEMATICS PROGRAM

Most children will enjoy their first-grade mathematics activity and will learn number ideas and facts quickly. The good program is one that stimulates your child's thinking, that tickles his curiosity and challenges him to use his mind. If the answers to most or all of the following questions are yes, chances are your child is participating in an effective program. If many answers are no, you may want to inquire further about the program by talking with your child's teacher and, possibly, the principal.

What to Look for in the Classroom

When you visit your child's classroom, do you see

- Number lines displayed on the walls or on the floor?
- Graphs of many kinds on many subjects, reflecting work that the teacher and the class have done?
- Chips, counters, Cuisenaire rods, and similar objects used for counting and sorting?
- Jars or other containers of beans, peas, or marbles used for estimating?
- Math workbooks (of more than one kind) located where children can use them readily?

- Worksheets done by children, showing good work that they have done?

What to Look for From the Teacher

Does your child's first-grade teacher

- Describe clearly what the class has been doing in mathematics and what she plans for it to do?
- Provide time each day, or at least on most days, for mathematical activity?
- Provide time and opportunity for the children to learn and practice using number facts?
- Provide time and opportunity for the children to understand the mathematical ideas and relationships they are learning?
- Use concrete objects to help children understand mathematical ideas?
- Know your child's individual abilities and feelings about mathematics?
- Show enthusiasm about teaching mathematics?

What to Look for From Your Child

In the course of the first-grade year, does your child

- Seem interested in numbers, quantities, and mathematical relationships?
- Show a sense of excitement and confidence in using his mind for math?
- Describe math activities he has done in class?
- Bring home papers or worksheets reflecting work that he has done?
- Seem able to do the work listed in "The Signs of Progress"?

HOW TO HELP YOUR CHILD AT HOME

Under normal circumstances, most schools will do a good job of teaching mathematics to your first-grade child. With a little time and patience, you can reinforce at home what your child is learning at school. But remember, unless you can be consistently encouraging and supportive, you are better off doing nothing. An anxious or impatient parent does not help to build the confidence your child needs at this age.

Do's

- Praise and encourage your child's efforts to "use mathematics": to count, to estimate, to measure, to use numbers.
- Use concrete objects to help your child develop confidence in counting. For example, ask your child to count the cookies on the plate, the dishes on the table. Rearrange the objects and ask your child to count them again.
- Practice estimating with your child. Ask, "Which is taller, the lamp or the coat rack?"
- Practice measuring with your child. Use rulers, yardsticks, and nonstandard units of measurement—handsbreadth, shoe lengths, newspaper widths. Measure objects longer than the measuring instrument, and talk about what to do when there are fractions "left over."
- Make a floor plan of your house or apartment with your child. Your child can measure the distances while you write them down.
- Discuss time with your child. Get beyond mere telling time with questions like, "If we want to be at Grandma's at six o'clock, and it takes forty-five minutes to get there, what time should we leave?"

Don'ts

- Don't be impatient. If your child seems slow to learn, it is not because he wishes to be slow. Besides, the problem may be yours, not his. If your ego is on the line, back off.
- Don't persist with an activity or a game if your child becomes frustrated or inattentive.
- Don't say that you (or some people) are just "no good at math." Almost everyone can learn first-grade mathematics. Don't foster a defeatist attitude.
- Don't suggest that girls aren't as good in math as boys.
- Don't criticize the teacher's way of doing things. To learn well, your child must have confidence in his teacher. Besides, the way you were taught is not necessarily the right way.

THE SIGNS OF PROGRESS

By the time they leave the first grade, children who are making normal progress in mathematics should have mastered most of the curriculum described above. At minimum, children should be able to do the following.

Numbers and Numeration

- Compare sets of objects with more, less, and the same amounts. Match number words and symbols with sets of objects from zero to twenty.
- Count the cardinal numbers from 1 to 100. Count forward and backward by ones, twos, and fives on a number line.
- Read and write numerals from 1 to 100. Understand the meaning of each digit in two-digit numbers.

Operations With Whole Numbers

- Group concrete objects by twos, threes, fives, tens. Understand the concept of even and odd numbers.
- Demonstrate knowledge of addition and subtraction facts through 10.
- Add three numbers that sum to 10 or less.
- Add and subtract two two-digit numbers that do not require regrouping (carrying).
- Read and write number sentences using the symbols + and − both horizontally and vertically.

Operations with Fractions

- Divide a whole object into equal parts (halves, thirds, fourths, fifths).
- Divide a set of objects into equal parts (halves, thirds, fourths, fifths).
- Read and write fractions with a numerator of 1 and a denominator of 1–9.

Probability and Statistics

- Collect, organize, and record information using two or more categories at a time.
- Tally the information obtained by data gathering and graphing, and compare the amounts in each category.

Geometry and Measurement

- Make rough estimates and comparisons of size, distance, weight, capacity, temperature, time.

- Measure lengths in centimeters and inches.
- Measure time using calendars and clocks.
- Measure weight in pounds and kilograms.
- Measure capacity in quarts, pints, and liters.
- Demonstrate an awareness of geometric shapes, patterns, and designs.

Most children acquire these skills by the end of the first grade. If your child fails to do so, you should talk with the teacher or the principal to hear their views of the nature of the problem. Perhaps your child is simply developing more slowly than some; perhaps there are signs of a learning problem that needs attention; perhaps the curriculum is so organized that your child will learn the skills in second grade.

Some children make progress beyond the normal. Again, if your child shows unusual proficiency, you may wish to talk to the teacher to see what adjustments, if any, should be made in his second-grade program and to obtain suggestions for how you can enrich your child's experience at home.

Writing in the First Grade

During the past decade, the teaching of writing has enjoyed a renaissance. The actual process of writing has been observed, evaluated, analyzed, and reanalyzed. Professionals have examined what they do and assigned names to the steps of the process. Children are then taught to follow these steps. The idea is to help children master the process of writing rather than to focus solely on the product. The method is commonly called the *process approach.*

THE WRITING PROCESS

Before they do anything else, writers think about what they plan to write. Often they think a long time before they actually decide on a subject. They may or may not talk about the subject with others. They may or may not do research on their subject. This step is called *rehearsal,* or *pre-writing.*

Next, the writer makes a rough first attempt, similar to the first rough sketches an artist makes. Researchers of the writing process call this step *drafting.* Content is of primary importance during this part of the process. Handwriting, spelling, and punctuation are not. This is the composing step. Often a writer calls the product of this step his *rough draft*.

Next the writer may read his work himself, and/or he may read it to others: his editor, a friend, his writing workshop—an audience. The audience will ask questions like, "What do you mean here? I wish you would tell me more about this. You are covering too long a time period. I wish you could tell me how the house smelled after the fire," or "Perhaps you might start the story with dialogue."

At this point in the process, a skilled audience or critic will not say, "Your handwriting is sloppy" or "You spelled *nite* wrong." That sort of criticism is disheartening and does nothing to improve the content of the writing.

After the audience has made comments, the writer evaluates the comments and *revises* his work. He adds descriptions, he deletes passages, he adds passages, he moves passages around. He may eliminate the beginning paragraph or delete the last two sentences.

When he is sure that his work says what he wishes it to say, he adds the final touches, by *editing*. He checks his spelling and punctuation, recopies his work, and types it or asks someone else to type it.

In general, the writing process applies to all writers. Individual differences do enter the picture, since writing is a creative and personal endeavor. There is, however, enough general agreement about the broad steps of the writing process to help teachers teach writing better.

THE FIRST-GRADE WRITER

The first-grade writer is on the threshold of his writing career. His early experience with writing may determine a lifelong attitude. He should be treated with great care by you and his teacher.

The first grader's school time is filled with speaking, reading, and writing activities. Speaking and reading both serve as preparation and enrichment for the writing he does. One popular writing activity in which children participate is group writing. The entire class composes a story that the teacher writes on poster paper. During such activity the children learn about the drafting process with none of the frustration. The teacher spells and does the handwriting. The children do nothing but draft or compose. The children also observe the teacher using proper punctuation and spelling. Since learning usually takes place from example, this is a very important activity.

In one first-grade class, the teacher read a story to the class about a little girl who moved to a new house. In September, the class talked about how they would feel if they were the little girl. Then as a group they wrote the following story, dictating it to the teacher, who helped them refine their sentences and organize their thoughts:

> We moved into a new house. I felt sad because I couldn't see my friends anymore because we were far away. We built a platform on the side of the new house. The house is big. We painted it white and blue. We like the new house.

Most first graders still begin their writing with artwork. Drawings enable them to focus, make a choice of topic. As they draw, they add certain details and leave others out. They are telling a story in their drawing, a story they will later relate in words. Sometimes, even before they draw, they talk with a friend or the teacher about what they plan to draw, what moment of their life they choose to memorialize. This is all part of the rehearsal step.

In one first-grade class the children write a special story about a particular child each week. One week it was Jonathan's turn.

One girl drew a picture of the teacher and wrote under the drawing, "Jon lks His Tichru a Lit." Underneath, the teacher wrote, "Jon likes his teacher a lot."

Another child wrote, "I Lac Jonathan Be cas he has a Game cad arrntine." The teacher wrote "because" under "Be cas," "called" under "cad," and "air hockey" under "arrntine."

As the first-grade year progresses, drawings become less important, often becoming illustrations that are added when the story has been completed. By the end of the first grade, for many children the first draft is all text. For some, drawings continue to be important in the drafting process. (One young writer the authors know well continued to add little mouse illustrations in her first drafts right through high school.)

The drafting step is perhaps the most important stage in the writing process. It is the true time of composing. It is a difficult step for first-grade children, who are just learning the physical skill of handwriting. The pencil is difficult to hold, letters are difficult to form, and first graders have so much to say. Sometimes, the length of their stories is limited by how much they can physically write rather than how much they have to say. The teacher or aide who offers a helping hand with writing a long story is often wise. If a child finds the physical act of writing an overwhelming burden because of a learning disability or a developmental lag, he should still have the opportunity to "write" his story. Difficulty in handwriting is not related to a lack of writing ability, although many adults think the two are the same.

When given the freedom to select topics, first-grade children choose things that are close to them—stories about their families, friends, pets, a recent holiday. Sometimes they write about favorite characters in books or on television. In general, first graders' written pieces may range from a few sentences to a few pages. Their writing sounds like their spoken words. There is a strong relationship between the voice they use when they speak and the voice they use when they write.

One little first-grade girl wrote:

My mommy is havige a beby in Five mutes.
I am so aksidid.
I dot kere if itisa boy ore a grie at lest it is a hlthy baby
I am going totak gode kere ure the beby I kete wete in-
tile the beby cums awte uve my mommy's tumye

Under each misspelled word, the teacher wrote the correct
one.

Another first-grade child wrote a book about her sister. The
first page of her ten-page illustrated book resembled Figure 1.

In first grade, punctuation is usually absent, with periods and
capitals occasionally appearing, usually where they don't belong.
Drafts often contain both uppercase and lowercase letters. Sometimes, first-grade children will use capital letters, periods, and
apostrophes, but punctuation is not a priority for them.

Revision is a task that is taught in first grade, but first graders
do it in only the most basic way. The teacher and members of the
class may make suggestions to a child, asking him to add more to
his story or perhaps sequence it differently. The teacher can show
him how to cut and Scotch-tape, thus enabling him to move text
around without recopying.

Editing is usually done by the teacher in the first grade so that
the final piece is spelled correctly and the punctuation is accurate.
If a word processor is used, revision and editing become easy
tasks, because there is never copying over and all the young
writer's energy can be directed at improving the quality of his
piece. By the end of the year, edited first-grade writing should
look like this:

ME AND KATIE

Kate is my sister. She is nice. I really love her. But
sometimes I hate her.

One day Katie broke something and it broke one of my
privileges.

Sometimes Kate gets me in hot water.

Kate is my sister. She is nice. I rely really love her. But some— times I hate her.

Figure 1.

Sometimes Katie splashes me in the tub!

Here is a picture of Katie.

I really really really really really really really really
really really really really really really really really really
really really really really really really love her!

The End

SPELLING AND HANDWRITING IN THE FIRST GRADE

Spelling is inventive. Children depend on their phonetic sense for the most part. Occasionally a teacher will have to ask a child to identify a word because the spelling is so remote from the actual word. Good teachers choose words from children's writing for spelling lessons. If a child wishes to use a word in his writing, he is motivated to spell it correctly. Children's spelling improves as their skill in reading and writing grows. Formal lessons in spelling aid this process, but most spelling knowledge comes from reading and seeing words over and over and then using them in writing. Some schools use textbooks for their spelling lessons, others use lists comprising words children use. Still others use a combination of the two.

Some children are natural spellers. It is easy for them. Others find it a difficult task all their lives. It is essential that you as a parent understand that your child will spell correctly because he will be a natural speller or because the teacher will help him in spelling lessons or because he will learn to use a dictionary. Likewise, he will learn grammar and punctuation as he grows. Right now, in the first grade, the important thing is the content of his writing. Your child must be encouraged to write more and more if he is to be a proficient writer later on in his life.

Most handwriting programs focus on legibility rather than on beauty. A beautiful hand is still appreciated, but the days when it was of prime importance are gone. In today's schools, teachers try to help children develop a handwriting that can be read easily. For most children, this will not be a problem. For some, it may be close to impossible. For those few, word processors and type-writers will bring salvation.

Most first grades use a particular writing program with a writing workbook. The teacher instructs the class on the black-board in the formation of letters and has the children practice with examples of good handwriting on the page in front of them.

Teachers encourage good writing habits: proper writing po-sitions, good posture, adequate lighting. Left-handed children should be given special instruction about the paper position: they should slant their paper from the right at the top to the left at the bottom (approximately two o'clock position). The pencil position is about the same for right-handed and left-handed children, al-though the latter sometimes hold the pencil farther from the point.

If you notice that your child is having difficulty with his handwriting, speak to the teacher and see what you can do to help. He may never have beautiful handwriting, but it is impor-tant that his writing be legible. Find out whether he is simply slow in developing his fine-motor coordination or whether he may have more severe problems. The chapter "The Child With Learn-ing Problems" may be helpful to you should his problem be se-vere.

A GOOD WRITING PROGRAM

A good writing program is one that

- Values children's experience and their perception of it.
- Encourages children to be good observers, to listen to sounds, to notice smell, to see detail.

- Helps children record the details they observe.
- Provides a writing center, a place where there are pencils and blank stapled books—a place where children may go if they wish to write.
- Provides time for the entire writing process, and time for children to listen to and read their classmate's writing. Some classrooms have libraries of "books" by classroom authors. Some schools have parent volunteer programs with parents editing and typing books by children.
- Teaches children how to be good editors, to ask the right questions, to be specific, to be positive and encouraging and yet helpful, to be committed to helping each author create a better piece.
- Recognizes the difference between handwriting and writing, helping children whose handwriting is an overwhelming task by allowing them to dictate occasional stories or use a word processor.
- Values literature, encourages children to read, provides time for reading aloud to them.
- Recognizes that writing, like speaking, is a trial-and-error skill and needs encouragement and nurturing.
- Displays children's writing prominently and attractively.
- Stresses the specifics of what is good about some writing samples.
- Shows interest in every child's writing.

During a lecture about writing instruction, a teacher in the audience once asked one of the authors, "What do you say when there is nothing good in a child's piece of writing? How can you be positive and still not lower your standards?"

The author answered that the best thing a teacher can do is show interest in the writing. Interest is perhaps the highest compliment. The teacher can ask questions about the content of the piece, can request more information. What is important is not to preface the interest by negative comments, such as "You didn't tell enough," "You ran on too much," or "I don't understand what you're trying to say." Rather, the teacher might start by saying, "I really want to know more about your story. Tell me . . ."

What You Can Do

You can help your child in a variety of ways. You can

- Act as a role model by writing yourself—letters, notes, whatever. Don't speak of writing as if it were an onerous task.
- Tell your child stories and encourage him to tell you stories.
- Help your child be a good observer. Talk about what both of you see, hear, and smell.
- Provide your child with a well-lit place to write and ample paper and pencils.
- Display your child's art and writing prominently in your home.
- Show interest in the stories your child tells and writes.
- Praise your child's writing efforts. Remember, he is just at the beginning of his writing career.

Encouragement for what is good will go a long way. Criticism for what is wrong is easy to give, but bears only the fruit of discouragement. You will not be lowering your standards if you find what is good and clap long and hard. Don't judge your child's writing efforts by adult standards. He is only a first grader. His spelling, punctuation, and handwriting will improve with time, practice, and instruction. So will his writing, with the teacher's and your interest and encouragement.

Social Studies in the First Grade

Later on, when children enter high school, their study of how people live and work together and relate to their natural environment is divided into separate academic subjects: history, geography, economics, anthropology, sociology, political science, and so on. Specific periods of the day are set aside to study these subjects, and often students are left on their own to make connections between these separate subjects and their other studies—not to mention their personal lives.

But in the first grade life is still all of a piece. By now most children have learned to work and play in a group, and they have a sense of themselves as both unique individuals and as people who share common characteristics with other people. They have a growing awareness of life and work in the larger community, although their sense of time and space is still closely linked to the here and now. They continue to be actively curious about the world around them, eager to explore the way things work and the way people live.

What they do as they pursue this curiosity cannot be neatly divided into subject areas. Sometimes it looks like reading or literature, sometimes like math or science, sometimes like history or geography, sometimes like all of these at once. In the language of the school, their social studies learning is *integrated* into other activities.

Across the country there is no consensus about what a good first-grade social studies program should contain. (Many social studies textbooks in widespread use do emphasize the study of the family at this level.) The skills and content to be mastered are much less specifically defined than they are in math or reading. What matters is that your child's own skills of social adaptation and understanding of how people live and work in the world beyond his family circle continue to grow.

THE FIRST-GRADE SOCIAL STUDIES CURRICULUM

Among the ideas (concepts) commonly taught in the first-grade social studies curriculum are those related to the family, community, and the country.

Family

- Most children live in families.
- Families differ in size, composition, and the work people do.
- Families eat different food, live in different houses, and wear different clothing, but share the need for food, shelter, and clothing.
- Family members work in different ways to meet their needs.
- Families must sometimes depend on others to help meet their needs.
- Family members learn from one another, from neighbors, and from others.

- Families must make decisions and solve problems.
- Families change as time passes.

Community

- Families live in communities to meet their needs, to get help, to have companionship.
- People in communities work at different jobs to do things that people in the community need.
- Communities have rules to protect people's health and safety.
- People in communities use tools to do their work.
- People in communities use money to buy the things they want or need.
- Communities provide services that families could not get alone.
- Communities change as time passes.

Nations

- Our nation is the United States of America.
- Our nation is a democracy, a "free country" in which "all men are equal."
- People in our nation celebrate certain national holidays, for example, Martin Luther King Day, Lincoln's Birthday, Washington's Birthday, Memorial Day, the Fourth of July.
- The flag is a symbol of our nation.
- The nation provides services that communities cannot provide alone.
- Our nation has changed as time has passed.

TEACHING THE FIRST-GRADE SOCIAL STUDIES CURRICULUM

Listing the ideas in this way makes them seem more weighty than they really are. Much of the teaching and learning is indirect, the incidental by-product of celebrating holidays, pledging allegiance to the flag, talking about things that happen at home, conducting classroom activity in a democratic manner. (Children's use of the ballots in the math lesson described on pp. 120–121 is itself a lesson in democracy.) Some of the teaching and learning is more direct—reading stories and drawing pictures about family life, visiting the post office and the fire station, listening to the policeman tell about the work he does, watching films or videotapes that show our world, our country, and our town from the air or from space. Almost always the teaching and learning are connected with something else the children are doing, a project or activity that involves language, science, mathematics, and art as well as ideas in social studies.

Most parents will recognize or remember classroom scenes like this:

An early afternoon in November, the week before Thanksgiving. The class has been studying native Americans, and the room is filled with Indian pictures and objects. Storybooks about Indians lie on the reading table; dried corn and colorful headdresses adorn the door; on the bulletin board are pieces of colored paper, each matching an Indian name ("Morning Star," "Fresh-Tracks-in-the-Snow") with the name of a child in the class; in the corner stands a magnificent seven-foot tepee, constructed of slats and heavy paper by the teacher's husband.

Some of the children are at their desks, drawing pictures and writing stories about what their families will be doing on Thanksgiving. (A parent volunteer works with them, writing down the words they want to use when they have trouble with them.) Later, these stories will be shared with the rest of the class.

This group of children is rehearsing a play about an Indian family at Thanksgiving. (The teacher has written it with help from the class.) The children take turns playing the various roles: brave, squaw, grandfather chief, small child, Pilgrim maid, and so on. One girl has a doll strapped to her back in a blanket, in the manner of a papoose; another girl plays the part of a brave. The children are having fun, but the atmosphere is serious, purposeful—in their imaginations they *are* native Americans.

When the rehearsal is over, the teacher gathers the entire class together and reads a story about an Indian family. Afterward, she and the class discuss it. "How did you feel when Little Bear was lost?" "Did you know that the Indians lived *right here,* where our school is?" "What do you suppose it was like then?" "How are our families the same as the Indian family? How are they different?"

Still later, the children draw pictures and write Indian stories of their own.

WHAT TO LOOK FOR IN A GOOD FIRST-GRADE SOCIAL STUDIES PROGRAM

As with the kindergarten, the specific contents of the first-grade social studies program is not important. What matters is that children continue to learn the skills and attitudes of constructive social behavior, enlarge their understanding of how other people live and work in the community and in the larger world, and expand their sense of place and time. Here are some things to look for:

• Does the teacher say your child is respectful and cooperative in his school behavior?

- Does the teacher say your child enjoys the company of other children and that he works and plays well in a group?
- Does your child show curiosity about your own and other families—how they are the same and different from your own?
- Does your child show curiosity and understanding about the way things work in your community: stores, subways, the post office?
- Does your child show increasing curiosity and understanding about times past and people who live elsewhere?
- Does your child bring home stories or pictures, or objects he's made, that reflect social studies activity, such as materials relating to a current holiday?

If the answers to questions like these are yes, your child is making normal progress. If the answers are no, you should make an appointment to see your child's teacher. Perhaps your child is experiencing a problem of growth and adjustment, or perhaps a hint from you will prompt the teacher to enrich her program.

Science in the First Grade

A recent position statement of the National Science Teachers Association says that "science should be an integral part of the elementary school program. It should be used to integrate, reinforce, and enhance the other basic curricular areas so as to make learning more meaningful for children ... [and] a minimum of 1½ hours/week of science should be required."

We all know how important it is that our children become knowledgeable about science. Without such knowledge, they may not be able to participate fully in the society in which they will live. But in America's elementary schools, in the authors' experience, the amount of science taught and the quality of science instruction are at best spotty.

Fortunately, there are many fine elementary teachers of science and many good elementary science programs. However, some teachers seem uncomfortable teaching science and uncertain about using science-oriented activities as a base for teaching skills in language and mathematics. The chief task of the first-grade program is still to teach children reading, writing, and mathematics. But the truly good elementary school will offer your child a stimulating science program as well.

THE FIRST-GRADE SCIENCE CURRICULUM

In recent years, leading teachers and scholars have agreed that a good science program combines content (information) with process (scientific inquiry). They also agree that children should have experiences in the earth, life, and physical sciences, that the specific content of these experiences is unimportant provided the subject matter is taught well, and that these experiences can be integrated into other learning activities in reading, language development, and mathematics.

Good teachers at this level continue to nurture children's natural curiosity about the physical world around them. They have children care for animals, grow plants, collect and compare rocks and leaves, watch and chart the weather. Children learn that all plants and animals have certain needs and that plants and animals depend on other plants and animals to provide these needs. They learn that objects have properties (for example, weight, color, texture, hardness, transparency) and that these properties can be changed (for example, by heat, cold, light, motion). They observe and identify change in living things, and they come to recognize patterns in life cycles and natural events.

At the same time, good teachers help children develop the skills and attitudes of scientific inquiry. Children learn to observe closely, to classify objects and events, to make rough measurements, to record and graph data. They begin to interpret what they experience and to establish connections between objects, events, and conditions.

TEACHING THE FIRST-GRADE SCIENCE CURRICULUM

The specific content of the science curriculum varies widely. Children work with plants, animals, fish, eggs, seeds, roots, butterflies, sand, water, soil, wood, metal, plastic, magnets, cloth—things indoors, things outdoors, things outdoors brought in (the crust of ice on the puddle), and things indoors taken out (the geranium placed on the windowsill in the cold). Typically, there is little uniformity from one classroom to another, even in the same school. Nor should there be: what matters at this age is that teacher and children work with things they find interesting and that they do so in a way that encourages scientific observation and thinking. The quality of the experience is what counts, not its sameness from one room to another.

Sometimes these science experiences grow naturally out of things that "just happen" in the classroom—the eggs hatch, the seed sprouts through the soil. Sometimes they are single lessons taught by teachers: the children blow up balloons in the warm classroom, take them outside into the cold air and watch them shrink, bring them back inside and watch them expand again. What a problem for young minds to tackle!

Sometimes they are more sustained units of instruction, at which children spend days or even weeks. Once we saw a rubbery skinlike flat gray substance on the floor of a Midwestern classroom. As part of the unit "Pioneers," the children were studying the food people used to eat. The question arose, what did people do without refrigerators? In October, the teacher brought an eighty-pound pumpkin to class. The children touched it, smelled it, tried to lift it, weighed it. They recorded their observations. Each day they examined it again, smelled it, weighed it, recorded the data on a graph. As the weeks passed, the pumpkin began to shrivel, dry, weigh less. What was happening? Many ideas were suggested and discussed. Our visit was made before the problem was solved, but we are sure that the children in this class will never forget the rotting pumpkin, that they have come to understand the importance of refrigeration in today's world, and that they are now ready to understand the phenomenon of dehydration and the abundance of water in living things!

WHAT TO LOOK FOR IN A GOOD FIRST-GRADE SCIENCE PROGRAM

A good first-grade science program continues to nurture your child's curiosity about the natural world and involves him in making the observations and comparisons that are fundamental to the scientific method. Here are some things you might look for:

• Does your child's teacher provide time for experiences in science?
• Are there plants, animals, rocks, soil, sand, water, and other interesting objects available in the classroom?
• Does your child actually use—handle, weigh, play with, inspect—these objects?
• Does some of your child's reading and writing relate to science?
• Does your child show curiosity about his natural environment at home and when you travel?
• Does your child feel good about using his mind and senses to explore new phenomena?

SECOND GRADE

The Second-Grade Child as a Learner

By the time most children enter the second grade, they have acquired most of the rudimentary skills they will need to function effectively throughout their years of schooling. They know how to play and work in a group—to take turns, to follow the rules, to share toys and implements, to cooperate with one another at a game or learning task. They are beginning to learn to read; for many, the emphasis will shift from decoding words to reading for comprehension. They are less egocentric than when they were younger, more in touch with the thoughts and feelings of the adults and other children around them.

As they progress through the second grade, they are wonderfully open to new experiences. They want to know all they can about the world they read about in books and watch on television. They are aware of current events: the child whose biggest story the preceding year was the family trip to Florida now talks about the latest space launch. They sponge up stories, music, poetry. They are proud of what they are learning, and eager to learn more.

As they move into Piaget's stage of concrete operations, they increasingly understand numbers and relationships, they communicate more easily, and they deal more readily with the ideas of past and future. They tend still to be somewhat literal in their thinking and not yet ready for the abstract logic they will acquire later. But they are already skilled and confident learners for their years, experienced, full of energy, and ready for more.

Reading in the Second Grade

THE IMPORTANCE OF READING

"Based on what we now know, it is incorrect to suppose that there is a simple or single step, which, if taken correctly, will immediately allow a child to read. Becoming a skilled reader is a journey that involves many steps. Strengthening any one element yields small gains. For large gains, many elements must be in place." Thus, *Becoming a Nation of Readers*, a Report of the Commission on Reading published in 1985, emphasizes the cumulative nature of learning to read. Although most children have begun formal instruction in reading, instruction in second grade continues to be crucial. The fact that your child has started on the road to learning does not mean his journey is over. Actually, it has just begun.

Children in second grade vary in their ability to read, and a good teacher will organize her reading program appropriately. Some children at the beginning of second grade are skillful at decoding and have developed a vocabulary of sight words. Others are on the brink of reading, and second grade will be the year when they truly become readers.

Reading at home continues to be as important as ever. Even your own reading for pleasure is important, for you are your child's most important role model. Play word games with your child, explain new words to him, go to the library together, choose books for yourself after he has chosen his, talk about some of the books you loved when you were a child. By talking with him you will help his vocabulary and his conceptual understanding to grow. All of these experiences will help him develop as a reader. Read together and nurture his growing skill with warm encouragement. Find a book that has chapters and read a new one at a special time each day.

WHAT IS READING?

True reading involves comprehending the meaning of the text and relating it to what the reader already knows. The report of the Commission on Reading says, "Reading is a process in which information from the text and the knowledge possessed by the reader act together to produce meaning. Good readers skillfully integrate information in the text with what they already know." The definition suggests the value of enriching the experience of your child. The richer his background, the more wealth he can bring to his reading experience. Reading is a great deal more than the mechanical process of decoding. Making judgments, predicting outcomes, understanding cause and effect, are all part of the total process of reading. Learning to read is a continuous process, one skill building on another. Indeed, it is a skill we must develop throughout our lifetime.

Reading is part of a child's total language development—listening, speaking, writing, reading. It builds naturally on the language capacity that the child already has. This is as true of the second- and third-grade child as it is of the first grade child. He moves gradually from known words to unknown words, and through speaking, listening, and reading he enlarges both his oral and his reading vocabulary. Always he should try to get the meaning of a passage as well as to recognize the words, relating what he reads to his own experience. Eventually, he learns to interpret what he reads—to describe the main idea, to locate key details, to identify cause/effect relationships, to make inferences.

The beginning years of learning to read are crucial. They should provide a strong foundation in skills and a positive attitude toward the pleasure and power of reading well. What do teachers do in the second grade to provide your child with a strong foundation in reading skills and an attitude that will prepare him for a life of enjoyable reading?

READING IN THE BEGINNING OF THE SECOND GRADE

The purpose of the reading program in the second grade is to reinforce and extend the basic word recognition and comprehension skills learned in the first grade. In grades three or four the program undergoes a striking change—in traditional terminology from "learning to read" to "reading to learn." Although the purposes, methods, and materials of instruction in second grade are essentially similar to those of first grade, many children experience a quantum leap in their reading ability during second grade.

During the summer between the first- and second-grade years many children seem to forget many of the reading skills they learned the year before. These skills tend to return quickly when children have the chance to use them again. For this reason many second-grade teachers begin the year with two to three weeks of diagnostic testing and review. Parents should understand the importance of this and not regard it as a "waste of time."

Toward the end of the second or third week of school, the teacher will have determined each child's appropriate instructional level and will begin to form reading groups. The instructional range in a typical second-grade class extends from readiness to well above grade level. Because the teacher's job is to help each child reinforce and expand his own reading skills (not to teach to the "average" level of the class), she must employ a wide variety of reading books and instructional materials. She must continue to teach skills begun in the first grade, as well as introduce new ones.

In a class involved in a basal reading series program, one group might begin the year by reviewing the skills taught in the level 1 reader and progress through the stories and exercises in the 2:1 and 2:2 readers (the readers for the first and second half of the second grade year) by the end of the year. Another group, not yet ready for the 2:1 reader, might work at readiness or level 1 in a basal series they did not use in first grade. (In this way the stories and pictures would not be familiar to them, but they would continue to work with material of appropriate difficulty.) A third group, more advanced, might use portions of the 2:1 and 2:2 readers and move to the 3:1 reader by midyear. Of course, children in all three groups might be involved in other learning tasks to supplement those provided in the basal reading program. Because of the extended range of instructional needs, one is apt to see a more varied combination of instructional techniques and materials in second grade than in first grade.

HOW DO TEACHERS TEACH CHILDREN TO READ IN SECOND GRADE?

In the beginning of second grade, children's skills in reading vary greatly. Some children have become quite expert, while others still need very basic instruction. The basic decoding skills that were introduced in first grade continue to be taught in second grade. The two reading skills emphasized in second grade are word recognition and comprehension.

Word Recognition Skills

In order to have a firm foundation in reading, children are taught *sight word* skills and *word attack* skills. Sight word skills allow readers to recognize a word instantly, without a moment's hesitation. Word attack skills give readers the tools to unlock the meaning of (or *decode*) unfamiliar words. Among the word attack skills are the use of configuration clues, picture clues, context clues, phonic analysis, and structural analysis.

Sight Word Skills

By the beginning of second grade, most children have acquired a fairly large number of sight words. Their bank of sight words makes reading a little less arduous than it was in the beginning of first grade, and their sight word resources were limited, if they existed at all. With continued exposure to reading and writing, the second grader's sight word list grows steadily.

Word Attack Skills

CONFIGURATION CLUES

The shape of a word, like *octopus*, or the presence of a double letter, like the two *o*'s in *book*, is helpful to the beginning reader, and your child may be such a reader when he starts second grade. However, since many second graders are well into reading, the use of configuration clues diminishes quickly.

PICTURE CLUES

Also helpful to the beginning reader are picture clues. If the story is about a monkey and there is a picture of a monkey, the young reader will use the picture clue to get the word *monkey*, which will then be added to his sight word list because of its configuration. Like the use of configuration clues, picture clues are only helpful to the beginning reader.

CONTEXT CLUES

The use of context clues is a skill that is employed throughout a person's reading lifetime. Most of us will guess the meaning of an unknown word by the context in which we read it. Identification of an unknown word in a sentence that is otherwise known is an important skill that is continually reinforced during second grade. A child who does not know the word *frightened* might be able to identify it within the sentence "The frightened pig hid under the bed when the wolf came to the door."

PHONICS

Phonics involves the relationship of letters to sounds. Beginning readers learn to recognize letters and groups of letters. They learn to associate the appropriate sound with each letter or letter group and to blend the separate sounds together to form a word. The ability to see letter-sound relationships enables a child to break the code, or *decode*, a multitude of words he might not be able to read otherwise. The second-grade reading curriculum usually includes the following within its phonics program:

- Consonant sounds if the child has not yet learned them.
- Consonants in an initial position in a word (*b*ox), final consonants (boa*t*), and medial consonants (la*t*er).
- Consonant blends and digraphs (*dr*aw, *ch*in).
- Consonants that have two sounds (*c*an, *c*ent; *g*ive, *g*entleman).
- Short and long vowel sounds (h*a*t, l*a*te).
- Silent letters (*g*naw, bom*b*).
- Three-letter initial clusters (*str*ipe, *spr*ing).

- Word families (*fan, can, man, tan; hot, spot, cot*)
- Function of *y* as a consonant or a vowel (*young, baby*).

Although most reading experts agree that phonics offers a marvelous tool to the reader, few believe that phonics should be taught exclusively. It is important to remember that phonics is a means to an end, which is reading, not an end in itself. The report by the Commission on Reading suggests that phonics be introduced early in the child's reading career, that it be kept simple, and that it be completed by second grade unless individual needs indicate otherwise.

STRUCTURAL ANALYSIS

Another way to approach reading is by analysis of the word. Structural analysis includes seeing small words in big words, recognizing prefixes and suffixes, learning that words can be broken up into pieces or syllables, recognizing common endings such as *-ed, -ing, -er,* and *-est.* The standard structural analysis skills taught in the second grade include the ability to:

- Recognize little words in big words.
- Recognize compound words (*birthday, campground*).
- Understand possessives.
- Understand contractions.
- Find root words within longer words.
- Separate words by syllables.
- Alphabetize by first and second letters.

Comprehension Skills

All the word attack skills in the world are of no use if a reader has no understanding of what he is reading. Although the ability to pronounce an unfamiliar word and know what it means in isolation is certainly important, understanding written passages is what reading is really all about. Some studies of American readers have revealed that the teaching of comprehension skills has been a weak spot in primary education. Therefore, teachers at the primary level are trying to remedy the problem by stressing comprehension skills from the beginning of a child's reading career.

Comprehension skills taught in the second grade usually include the following:

- Discerning multiple meanings of words (*race*).
- Recognizing synonyms—words that mean the same (*laugh, chuckle*).
- Recognizing antonyms—words that mean the opposite (*hot, cold; good, bad*).
- Recognizing homonyms—words that sound the same (*sun, son*).
- Drawing conclusions.
- Predicting outcomes.
- Finding proof.
- Associating written passages with illustrations.
- Following printed directions.
- Finding the main idea.
- Following the sequence of plot.
- Using table of contents, titles, and page numbers.
- Finding specific information.
- Summarizing written passage.
- Recognizing cause and effect.

The growing list of skills taught in the second grade reveals the continuous and cumulative nature of reading. Each grade and each skill builds on one that is already part of a child's repertoire, with the ultimate goal being the understanding and appreciation of written passages.

Appreciation of Literature

The love of literature gives lifelong pleasure. Early exposure to good writing starts a young reader on the right path. Reading aloud by parent and teacher should begin before the child can read and continue long after. Although most basal readers now include selections from fine literature, the effective teacher enriches her program with a variety of quality children's literature.

Literature appreciation skills are an extension of comprehension skills. Among the appreciation skills taught in second grade are:

- Dramatizing stories that have been read.
- Illustrating stories that have been read.
- Distinguishing between reality and fantasy.
- Recognizing humor.
- Recognizing poetry and imagery.
- Discerning plot, characterization, and setting in a story.
- Recognizing mood in a poem or story.

Your school librarian or public librarian will help you find good books to share with your child. Make visits to the library a regular outing with your child. You can help to nurture your child's growing appreciation of literature.

(A suggested reading list appears at the end of the book.)

BASAL READERS

Basal readers are used by the large majority of school districts in the country. Usually, the series is chosen by the district and the same series is employed throughout the whole district. In some districts, the school will choose the series. In a small number of school districts, the grade-level teachers or the individual classroom teacher will select the series. In a very few cases, the classroom teacher will design her own program, with minimal reliance on a basal reader.

Basal reading programs include extensive materials that are organized to teach in a graded way all the skills needed for reading. Programs include readers, workbooks, teacher's manuals, and a variety of supplemental materials, such as audiotapes, posters, supplemental readers, and dolls. Teacher's manuals provide detailed instructions about how to proceed with each lesson to ensure that all skills are covered. The following excerpts are from the Teacher's Edition of *Riding Rainbows*, part of Allyn and Bacon's *Pathfinder* series.

FOLLOW-UP DISCUSSION AFTER READING

When pupils have read the entire story, choose questions from the following to guide a discussion.

1. Would you have wanted to trade places with Mary? Why or why not? (valuing—personal judgment, applicative)

2. What do you think was the most difficult part of Mary's life? (valuing—personal judgment, interpretive)

3. Why is school important in a person's life? (valuing—personal judgment, interpretive)

ACTIVITIES FOR SKILL DEVELOPMENT AND EVALUATION

From the suggestions below, choose activities to meet the needs of your pupils. Evaluate pupil achievement throughout the lesson. Activities marked with [E] are especially suited for evaluation. Activities marked with [I] may be completed independently.

Objective 1: Decoding: To decode words that contain the grapheme-phoneme correspondences *ear/ər/ and ear/ir/,* as in the words *learn* and *ear.*

Activity. Write the following sentence on the board:

Earl said, "I'll have to get up early to earn the money to buy a pearl."

Read the sentence and ask pupils to listen to the vowel sounds in the underlined words. Ask pupils if they all have the same vowel sounds. Have someone identify the three letters that stand for the vowel sounds.

Next, write the sentence below on the board:

Said the brand new car,
"Oh <u>dear</u>, how I <u>fear</u>
that what I <u>hear</u> means
I must be out of <u>gear</u>."

Read the sentence again and ask pupils to listen to the vowel sounds of the underlined words. Have the three letters that stand for the vowel sounds in each word underlined. Help pupils verbalize that the letters *ear* can represent the sounds heard in *learn* or the sounds heard in *ear*. Ask pupils to read the following words, trying each of the sounds if necessary:

| dear | fear | heard |
| learn | smear | gear |

Discuss the meanings of the words.

Basal reading programs are organized around a scope and sequence of skills, each skill building on the next, each reading book building on the previous one and increasing in difficulty. Should a child finish a reader but not be ready to begin the next level of difficulty, the program offers supplemental readers on the same level as the one just completed. Vocabularies in basal series are controlled and limited and are usually within the speaking and listening vocabulary of the child.

In the past, basal reader series have been criticized for their dull stories about middle-class, sexist America. Although many of the stories still reflect middle-class values, the publishers have made great strides toward including selections from good literature and stories about inner-city children who live in varied family situations.

Basal programs are designed to be complete reading programs, and many teachers rely on them totally. However, there are many ways to extend the scope of a reading program. Indeed, a creative and knowledgeable teacher can design a fine reading program in the second grade without the use of a basal series at all.

INDIVIDUALIZED READING PROGRAMS

In an individualized reading program, reading skills are taught using books selected by the students rather than the teacher. Some teachers employ an individualized reading program in place of a basal reading program. Others use it as a supplement to a basal series system. Many teachers use it as their students become more skillful readers.

Motivation is an essential ingredient. In the beginning of the year, the teacher may have displays of books for children who like sports, children who like fairy tales, and so on. She may read selections from books to pique interest or she may have children recommend books to one another. A teacher who runs an individualized reading program is usually full of ideas.

To conduct a good program, the teacher must be organized. The teacher must know each child's strengths and weaknesses as a reader. First-grade records, conversations with the first-grade teacher, reading tests, and a short conference with the child about what he has been reading and what he likes to read reveals a child's reading needs to an experienced teacher. The teacher should also know the child and his interests so that appropriate and interesting books can be suggested.

A large classroom library is almost a requirement for an individualized reading program. If district money is scarce, the school library or public library may lend books on a rotating basis for the classroom's use. Parent groups may purchase books for classrooms, and individual parents may donate books after their own children have read them. Local book fairs are often a wonderful source of second hand books.

The teacher should be familiar with the books in the classroom library so that she can make good recommendations. The school librarian and public librarian can be valuable sources as well.

Scheduling of individual time with each student is an important element of an individualized reading program. Teachers should help select books so that the reading level is neither too low nor too high for the child. During the conference, the teacher should check comprehension skills by asking questions about the story, and test word analysis skills by having the child read a passage orally. With good record-keeping, the teacher can design the skills lessons each child needs. Independent activities are prescribed when necessary. When a group of children need the same skill, group activities are organized.

Classrooms where individualized reading programs exist are lively places. They are often filled with stories children have written about books they have read, models of a vivid scene or episode from a particular story, or drawings of a favorite character. Such projects encourage children to read the books that have been enjoyed by their classmates. Peer recommendations and book sharing play a major role in an individualized reading program.

LANGUAGE-EXPERIENCE PROGRAMS

A language-experience approach in the classroom recognizes that the processes of thinking, writing, reading and speaking are interrelated. Basic to this approach is the belief that the child is most interested in his own experience and is likely to learn most quickly from it.

Most teachers who use a language-experience approach combine it with another teaching method: a basal system, an individualized reading system, or both.

Children's personal experiences are the foundation for the language-experience program. Children are encouraged to think, talk, and write about their experiences, their feelings, their thoughts. If they have problems writing, the teacher, an aide, or a volunteer writes what the child dictates. After the words are written down, the child's writing is used as his reading lesson. Often the words are difficult, for a child's spoken vocabulary is larger than his written one. Because the words have meaning, they are often learned despite their level of difficulty. Sometimes children keep their words on cards in their own private *word bank*. Each child's writing is shared with the other members of the class and becomes part of the curriculum for the class.

Language-experience programs often include group experience. If a holiday is approaching and some children are writing stories, the class may suggest words they would like to use in their stories. An easel in a classroom in November might have *Thanksgiving, turkey,* and *grandmother* written on a pad. The children may use the words in their writing, but they will also be learning to read them.

A child's story often becomes a book with several pages and illustrations. A little library is organized in the classroom so that children may read one another's books. This language-experience effort reflects a new approach to writing that is growing in popularity. We shall say more about it in the chapter on writing.

Books and trips are part of children's experiences, and the language-experience approach encourages children to write stories about favorite books, characters, and places.

Again, as with an individualized reading program, the teacher must assess each child's needs and arrange private conferences so that each child has the proper prescription of skills development. Worksheets that are either commercially produced or designed by the teacher are used in teaching the needed skills. If during conferences the teacher observes that a few children have a difficulty in common—perhaps with long vowels or consonant clusters (*br, dr, sc*)—she provides instruction and practice sessions for a group of children in that particular skill.

DIAGNOSTIC/PRESCRIPTIVE TEACHING

Diagnostic/prescriptive teaching should be part of all reading programs. If a teacher relies heavily on a basal series, the series will organize the scope and sequence of skills. Appropriate skills lessons are built into the prepared lessons in the teacher's guide and the workbooks, as well as in the supplemental materials. An effective teacher is aware of each student's particular needs. If a child needs help in certain skills, the teacher may have to provide additional instruction and material beyond what is offered in the basal series.

Many schools and school districts, whether or not they use a basal series system, have their own scope and sequence of skills, so that the teacher has some system against which to measure the progress of her students. In the rare school, it may be the teacher's responsibility to establish a hierarchy of skills for her students. Once this plan is established, the teacher evaluates each child through formal testing, informal conferencing, or both. Each child then has an evaluation, and prescriptions can be made according to need.

In most second grades, many children need help with the same skills; for these children, the teacher arranges class lessons or large group lessons. Some children may need specific help; for these children, the teacher designs lessons herself or uses commercially prepared ones.

Evaluation and follow-up of each child's skills development is as important as the original evaluation.

Reading for Fun

A teacher knows she has been successful when her students enjoy reading. A love of reading is a pleasure to be carried throughout one's life. The good primary teacher knows that she can help to instill that love in her pupils.

The classroom environment should be conducive to reading. Shelves of books, posters about books, and children's drawings and writing about books displayed attractively around the room make a difference. Cushions, chairs, reading alcoves, and comfortable spots for second graders to curl up with a good book establish good attitudes toward reading.

A positive relationship between the teacher and the school or public librarian can help a reading program. The teacher's enthusiasm about books and regular reading aloud to the class are also important ingredients.

The school should take advantage of its community resources. If authors of children's books live in the area, they are usually delighted to come speak to the children about their books. Parents' groups can hold book sales as fund-raisers. The more children see of books and people who love books, the more likely that they will become book lovers themselves.

Parents should share their love of books with their children. Reading aloud to your child each day will provide pleasure for both of you and establish a good feeling about reading in your child. By second grade, many children enjoy hearing a chapter a day from a longer book. Most libraries have lists of suggested books for children. Some of the authors' favorites are listed at the end of the book.

HOW DO TEACHERS ORGANIZE A SECOND-GRADE CLASS FOR READING INSTRUCTION?

There are many ways to organize a class for reading. Often a class's organization depends on the task at hand. Some lessons can be taught to the whole class, with practice following in small groups or individually. Some activities work well with only two children working together. At other times children work by themselves. As children develop and gain better reading skills, they become more independent. Consequently, most second-grade children are better able to work on their own than when they were in the first grade.

Teachers in most American second grades form reading groups as part of reading instruction. Although some teachers organize groups according to interests, most do so according to ability. The standard practice is to have at least three groups of children. The groups usually have between five and nine children. While the teacher works directly with one group, the other children may be involved in seatwork that has grown out of a previous lesson or be engaged in other activities.

Some schools form reading groups from the entire second-grade level or from all of the primary grades. Many schools involve the principal and the reading teacher with these groups. With such organization, more reading groups on different levels can be formed.

The grouping should grow out of evaluations made by the teacher at the beginning of the year. Children are aware of the hierarchy of the groups and their own placement. If they are in a low group, it can be a source of pain for them. If a child's reading improves, the teacher should be flexible enough to move him to a higher group when appropriate. Good teachers recognize that reading groups, although a good organization for teaching, can be difficult for the children in the lower reading groups.

They should try to provide activities for these children in which they can excel.

Some children in the lower group will never develop into good readers. They will learn to read, but reading may always remain somewhat of an arduous task. Others may simply be developmentally young and their reading skills may well come easily later, as they mature. If your child is on the low end of the reading scale, continue to encourage him. Read to him and be pleased with his progress even if it is slow.

Reading group time is an opportunity for both observation and instruction. The teacher can teach comprehension skills and word attack skills, as well as observe each child so that she can reinforce skills that need strengthening.

Some teachers, to keep children from feeling the stigma of being in a low reading group, place children in two groups: an ability group and an interest group. A child who is in a low-ability reading group may be very interested in horses along with some children in the middle- and high-ability groups. Twice a week, the interest group may meet, read, and share books about horses that are on different levels. The teacher's job is to know the children's interests as well as their reading levels, provide time for them to meet, and have books available on different levels that will meet their interests.

Some school districts who use one basal reading series will not allow their second-grade teachers to take the advanced readers past the second-grade-level basal reader because those children will be expected to read the third-grade reader the following year. If this is the policy, teachers should provide supplemental readers from the basal series, if they are available, or library books so that the good readers will not become bored. Many school districts have more than one series available so that teachers can take their more advanced readers beyond the second-grade level with basal readers from another series.

While a reading group is with the teacher, other children may be

- Working on a mural.
- Visiting the school library.
- Reading a library book.
- Writing a story.
- Playing a word game with a friend.
- Listening to a story on an audiocassette.
- Reading a story that another child has written.
- Conferencing with another child about a story one of them has written.
- Doing a worksheet that has grown out of a lesson.
- Reading a newspaper or magazine.

Workbook exercises can be helpful since some exercises reinforce important skills. Unfortunately, in many classrooms teachers rely on them for busywork, seatwork that is boring to children and offers little instructional value. In the good classroom, workbooks are only a small part of the many and varied activities used to teach reading.

Individual Differences

When an effective teacher arranges groups in her class, she tries to provide each pupil with learning opportunities that are suited to his reading level, developmental level, interests, and skills needs. Some educators feel that provision should also be made for the child's individual learning style.

Although there is no definitive research that tells us how each child learns best, we know there are differences in the way individuals learn. Some learn best visually; some through hearing. Some process information mentally; some need to handle objects or at least write things down. Some of us need to talk about what we're learning. Some proceed in sequential fashion from step 1 to step 2 to step 3; some prefer to jump into the middle of things. Some learn by investigation and discovery; others learn more quickly if material is presented in an organized fashion. Some require support; others require a challenge. Some work best alone, some with one other person, and some in small or large groups.

Obviously, each individual does not learn only one way and all learning models are appropriate at one time or another in a child's school career. The effective teacher provides many different ways of learning the material. When she sees how the child makes the most progress, she can provide more of that kind of work for him.

Children differ in their talents and interests. The effective teacher knows what these talents and interests are and helps her students develop them. One child may have hamsters at home and be willing to bring them to school the week that the teacher reads *The Great Hamster Hunt* by Lenore and Erik Blegvad to the class. Another child may collect shells and be willing to show them to the rest of the class after a visit to a local beach.

Some children find particular academic areas troublesome. One of our friend's children, a highly articulate second-grader, found it difficult to write his stories down. He had creative ideas but would often stop writing after a few lines. His teacher encouraged him to write as much as he could, but then allowed him to dictate the rest to a parent volunteer. His teacher's sensitivity to his particular difficulty helped him maintain his interest in creating stories.

WHAT TO LOOK FOR IN A GOOD SECOND-GRADE READING PROGRAM

The purpose of the reading program in the second grade is to reinforce and expand the skills taught in the first grade. The signs of a good second-grade program are much the same as those of a good first-grade program. In general, the teacher should know your child's individual needs and interests well, should provide skills instruction at an appropriate level of difficulty, and should involve your child in reading experiences that stimulate his curiosity and imagination. If your child is reading above grade level, you should find out what material the teacher is giving him to challenge his abilities and maintain his interest. If your child is progressing slowly, you should find out how the teacher is varying her approach to provide alternate ways of instruction that may be more effective. In doing so, remember that you and the teacher are partners in helping your child learn. Always indicate your willingness to help and make clear your desire to support the teacher's efforts.

What to Look for in the Classroom

When you visit your child's classroom, do you see

- Displays about books, children's stories, books written by children, posters about books, book jackets, a room in which reading takes place?
- Books for recreational reading that are attractively arranged and easily available to children?
- Chairs, cushions, and alcoves where children may read quietly?
- Audiotapes and tape recorders?
- An assortment of magazines, games, catalogs?

What to Look for From Your Child

Does your child

- Talk to you about the reading he has done at school?
- Show interest and enthusiasm about reading?
- Try to read the newspaper headlines?

- Bring home stories he has written in school?
- Look forward to your reading aloud to him?
- Show an understanding of the relationship between letters and sounds?
- Enjoy your trips to the library?
- Understand the stories you read together?
- Bring home puzzles or worksheets that show he is learning comprehension and word attack skills?
- Show signs of appreciation of literature?

What to Look for From the Teacher

When you talk to your child's teacher, does she

- Know your child's reading level, interests, attitudes toward reading, difficulties?
- Describe in detail the areas in which your child is showing progress as well as the areas in which he may be having difficulty?
- Show you the variety of materials she uses—basal readers, audiotapes, library books, workbooks, puzzles, games?
- Tell you about and show you samples of your child's work, as well as describe the general reading activities in class?
- Explain her general goals and her approach to the teaching of reading?

HOW TO HELP YOUR CHILD AT HOME

Although your child's reading instruction takes place in school, you can still be of invaluable help to him in his growing ability to read.

Do's

- Continue to praise and encourage your child's efforts to read.
- Make library visits a regular event.
- Tell your child when you are reading a book you particularly enjoy.
- Continue to read aloud to your child daily. If possible, read at a regular time. By now you and your child can be reading books that have chapters so that the life of the book extends over a longer time.
- Talk to your child about the story you are reading.
- Encourage your child to read to you when and if he wants to.
- Help your child with words only if he wishes you to. Let him read books to you that are easy for him so that he feels successful.
- Allow your child to read the same book more than once if he wishes. Children love a familiar book.
- Buy your child books as presents.
- Limit the amount of television your child watches and occasionally watch it with him so you will be able to talk to him about it.
- Talk with your child and help him to improve his vocabulary and concepts.
- Confer with your child's teacher at school periodically to learn about his progress.

Don'ts

- Don't force your child to read with you.
- Don't try to teach your child. Leave the formal instruction to the teacher.
- Don't criticize the teacher in front of your child. Speak to the teacher or principal if you are unhappy about how things are going.

- Don't expect your child to demonstrate his skills to you. Let him have fun reading with you.

THE SIGNS OF PROGRESS

By the end of the second grade, children should have mastered the fundamental word recognition and comprehension skills and should be able to apply them to reading material of increasing difficulty. If your child is reading at or above grade level by the end of this year, he has a solid reading foundation on which to build for the future. If he is not, you should undertake to find out why. Perhaps your child's rate of development is unusually slow; perhaps your child has a learning problem for which appropriate provision should be made; or perhaps the instruction he has received has been faulty in some way. You should confer with the teacher about your child's progress as the second-grade year progresses. But on no account should you leave a reading problem undiagnosed by the end of the second grade. (See the chapter "The Child With Learning Problems.")

Word Recognition Skills

By the end of the second grade, children making normal progress in reading should be able to

- Recognize, pronounce, and understand a sight vocabulary of about 500 words.
- Pronounce the appropriate sounds of single consonants, consonant clusters, and digraphs, vowels, and diphthongs.
- Blend letter sounds into words.
- Separate words into syllables.

- Separate roots from prefixes and suffixes.
- Use phonics clues, structural analysis clues, and context clues to identify unknown words.

Comprehension Skills

Given reading material on the second-grade level, your child by the end of the year should be able to

- Understand the meaning of sentences and paragraphs.
- Understand the main idea of a paragraph or short passage.
- Find significant details within a paragraph or passage.
- Recognize time intervals.
- Recognize cause and effect.
- Predict outcomes based on what is known.
- Follow simple directions.
- Solve simple problems.
- Distinguish fact from fiction.

Attitudes

By the end of the second year, your child should

- Enjoy hearing literature read aloud.
- Enjoy reading stories and poems.
- Feel positive about progress made in school.

Mathematics in the Second Grade

The songs of childhood suggest our youthful fascination with numbers.

> *One, two, buckle my shoe,*
> *Three, four, shut the door . . .*
>
> *This old man, he played one,*
> *He played nick-nack on my thumb . . .*
>
> *Forty-nine bottles hanging on the wall.*
> *If one of those bottles should happen to fall,*
> *There'd be forty-eight bottles hanging on the wall . . .*

If your second-grade child is lucky, he has not lost this fascination. Instead, his teachers and his parents have fueled his curiosity and kindled his imagination, helping him to use expressions of quantity to describe relationships in his environment. He has learned the concept of groups or sets, he can match and count objects, he can estimate and measure, he can count up and down in our number system, he knows and uses simple addition and subtraction facts. Above all, he understands the relationships between things and the numbers that describe them, and he has developed a growing confidence in the power of his mind to understand and use mathematics to solve problems in the world around him.

As we saw in the chapter "Mathematics in the First Grade," current thinking about good mathematics teaching emphasizes the importance of understanding mathematical principles, as well as the learning of facts by rote. The excessive formalism of the new math of the 1960s has been discarded, and ample time is provided for the instruction of basic skills. But good teachers know that these skills may never be used effectively if children are not taught how and when to use them. The goal of the mathematics curriculum is to help children acquire the ability to solve problems through the use of mathematics. For the second-grade child, as much as for his younger brother or sister, mathematics is not a set of facts to be memorized—it is an informed and disciplined activity of the mind.

The second-grade mathematics curriculum builds on the skills and knowledge taught in the first grade. By design, there is considerable repetition, as well as new material. Concepts and skills introduced in the first grade are reinforced in the second grade until the child masters them. (For this reason, you may wish to refer to the chapter "Mathematics in the First Grade.") Mathematics is a sequential and cumulative discipline, and children cannot climb the ladder securely if the lower rungs are shaky.

THE SECOND-GRADE MATHEMATICS CURRICULUM

Just as in the first grade, most second-grade mathematics curricula comprise five parts, or *strands:*

Numbers and numeration
Operations with whole numbers
Operations with fractions

Probability and statistics
Geometry and measurement

The sequence in which the curriculum is taught and the relative emphasis placed upon each part vary from school to school. But programs throughout the country are remarkably similar to one another.

The five main parts of the mathematics curriculum are taught throughout the elementary grades. In the second grade, the skills and knowledge that children should acquire are as follows.

Numbers and Numeration

- Counting—cardinal numbers: Learn to use cardinal numbers 1–1,000. Name the whole number immediately before and after any whole number from 1–999. Count forward and backward by ones, twos, threes, fours, and fives on a number line.
- Counting—ordinal numbers: Learn to use ordinal numbers to thirty-first or beyond.
- Numerals: Develop the ability to read and write numerals from at least 0–1,000. Recognize fraction numerals with numerators of 1–9 and denominators of 1–99. Recognize money notation to $100 or more. Group objects by tens.
- Place value: Use concrete objects and, later, pictures to represent numbers above 10. Understand the meaning of each digit in three-digit numbers: *Example* 673 = 6 hundreds, 7 tens, and 3 ones. Understand the meaning of zero in the place value system: *Example* 305 =

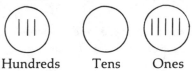

Hundreds   Tens   Ones

Use expanded notation for two- and three-digit numbers:

Example

36 = 3 tens + 6 ones = 30 + 6

243 = 2 hundreds + 4 tens + 3
ones = 200 + 40 + 3

Operations With Whole Numbers

* Addition and subtraction: Learn addition and subtraction facts through 18. Add and subtract two- and three-digit numbers without regrouping (carrying or borrowing):

Examples	72	796
	+16	−572
	88	224

Add and subtract two-digit numbers requiring regrouping:

Examples	72	64
	+18	−36
	90	28

Use addition and subtraction as inverse operations to check accuracy:

Examples	38	26
	−12	+12
	26	38

Understand that addition has the commutative property and that subtraction does not:

Example	12 + 4 = 4 + 12	YES
	12 − 4 = 4 − 12	NO

- Multiplication: Use arrays and number lines to understand multiplication as repeated addition:

$$\textit{Example} \quad \square\square\square\square$$
$$\square\square\square\square \quad 2 \times 4$$

Count on a number line by twos, threes, fours, fives, sixes, sevens, eights, nines, and tens to 100. Learn multiplication facts through 25.

- Division: Use arrays and number lines to understand division as repeated subtraction and as a process for finding the number of equivalent subsets of a given set:

$$\textit{Example} \quad \square\square\square\square$$
$$\square\square\square\square \quad 8 \div 2 = 4$$

Learn division facts through 25. Use multiplication and subtraction as inverse operations to check accuracy:

$$\textit{Example} \quad 24 \div 4 = 6 \qquad 6 \times 4 = 24$$

Understand that multiplication has the commutative property and that division does not:

$$\textit{Example} \quad 6 \times 3 = 3 \times 6 \qquad \text{YES}$$
$$6 \div 3 = 3 \div 6 \qquad \text{NO}$$

- Word problems: Use arithmetic knowledge and skill to solve simple word problems: *Examples:*   (1) Sixteen children prefer milk for lunch, and eleven children prefer juice. How many more children prefer milk than juice? (2) A teacher had eighteen cookies to share equally among six children. How many cookies did she give each child?

Operations With Fractions

- Equal parts of a whole: Divide whole objects into equal parts and relate part to whole (½, ⅓, ¼, ⅕, ⅙, ⅛, ⅒).
- Equal parts of a set: Divide sets of objects into equal parts and relate part to whole (½, ⅓, ¼, ⅕, ⅙, ⅛, ⅒). Find one half, one third, one fourth . . . of a collection of things.
- Number line: Locate halves on a number line and on a ruler.
- Ratio: Understand the concept of two-to-one correspondence:

Examples	two eyes—one face				
	two arms—one person				
	Number of children	1	2	3	4	5
	Number of legs	2	4	6	8	10

Probability and Statistics

- Data gathering and graphing: Collect, organize, and record information using two or more categories at a time. Arrange data in tables and graphs.
- Tallying: Tally the information obtained by data gathering and graphing. Compare the amounts in each category in terms of number, equality, and inequality.
- Sets: Make subsets of two or three things from larger sets of objects. *Example:* How many different sets of two can be made from a circle, a square, and a triangle?

Geometry and Measurement

- Estimating and making rough measurements: Continue concrete activities involving comparison of size, distance, weight, capacity, temperature, time. Make estimating an integral part of all measurement activity.

- Standard units of measure: Measure lengths in inches, feet, yards; in centimeters, decimeters, meters. Measure weight in ounces, pounds; grams, kilograms. Measure capacity in ounces, pints, quarts; deciliters, liters.
- Time: Tell time to the year, month, week, day, hour, minute, second (both analog and digital clocks).
- Temperature: Learn to read both the Fahrenheit and Celsius thermometers.
- Shapes: Continue to explore properties of two- and three-dimensional objects in the classroom and in the environment.

Problem Solving

The goal of the mathematics curriculum is to enable children to use mathematical thinking to solve real problems. Problem solving is not a mere adjunct to the curriculum; it is of the essence. Good teachers get children to use every portion of the curriculum to solve problems, and they teach the skills of problem solving openly and directly.

A *problem*, as the word is used here, should be distinguished from an *exercise*. An exercise is a task that the child already knows how to perform; for example, the teacher may assign exercises in subtraction in order to provide practice in computation. A problem is a situation or question that the child experiences as novel; since he does not yet know how to solve it, he must use logic and imagination.

Most problem-solving methods involve four steps.

1. *Understand the problem.* The child should repeat the problem in his own words, identify the key questions, and if necessary, write down the relevant facts.
2. *Make a plan.* Different problems require different plans. The child should draw upon his skills and knowledge to devise a

plan that may work. He may sort and classify, make tables or graphs and look for patterns, use pictures or charts, manipulate objects. Perhaps he will need his computational or measurement skills. Perhaps he will resort to trial and error. The trick is to make use of what he knows and not to jump to an easy answer that may be wrong or to give up because the problem seems hard.

3. *Carry out the plan.* Carrying out the plan is not the same as devising it. Often it is the step that requires putting pencil to paper and making computations.

4. *Check the answer.* Children should acquire the habit of first checking the *reasonableness* of the answer. (If the problem is to determine how many apples the class picked if each child picked four apples, and if there are twenty-five children in the class, it is *not* reasonable to say that the class picked twenty-nine apples.) Then they should check the *accuracy* of their answer.

Many good teachers talk about this four-step problem-solving method with their children and give them practice in following it.

TEACHING THE SECOND-GRADE MATHEMATICS CURRICULUM

By the time children enter the second grade, the patterns of school life have become comfortable and familiar. Specific routines vary from school to school and from classroom to classroom, but in general, children know that at a certain time they will have reading instruction, at another they will go to lunch, and at another they will study mathematics. In most second-grade classrooms, math is taught as a separate subject, usually in the morning, when the children are most alert. The teacher may work with the entire class, with a small group, or with one or two individuals, or she may vary the grouping to suit the task. She may relate the children's work in mathematics to other activity they have been conducting, or she may allow the math to stand on its own. She may teach in a direct, didactic fashion, explaining fully and leading the class along, or she may concentrate on helping the children to think things through for themselves. There is no one right style for every child and every situation. What is important, however, is that the teacher adhere to the fundamental principles listed below and that the tone of the activity be one that encourages the child to use his mind.

Consider these examples of effective teaching.

Late October. Halloween decorations abound. The teacher is working with a class of twenty-two, planning a Halloween party. She uses the party as a theme for a lesson on solving problems by using addition or subtraction. She asks, "If Lucy makes five peanut butter sandwiches and Larry makes five bologna sandwiches, how many sandwiches will we have for the party?"

A child immediately answers, "Ten."

"Good," she says. "How did you get ten?"

"I added five and five," says the child.

"Good," she says again. "If we bring ten sandwiches and eat eight of them, how many will we have left?" she asks. A child answers, and the teacher and the class discuss the answer. After several more questions and answers, the teacher says, "Sometimes you have to decide whether to add or subtract." The teacher distributes two worksheets to each child. The worksheets contain simple word problems requiring addition or subtraction for their solution: "Billy has 43¢. He gets 22¢ more. How much money does he have?" "There are 25 children on the bus; 12 get off. How many are left on the bus?"

The children work individually at these problems. The teacher circulates about the room, checking and helping. Some children finish before others. The teacher gives each of them a clean piece of paper with a number fact (for example, $19 - 12 = 7$) written at the top. She asks the children to make up and write down word problems to match their facts. Later, she asks the writers to read these problems to the class and helps the class solve them.

A cold day in January. A small group of children is working in the science corner, weighing and measuring rice. Most of the children are at their desks, filling out worksheets. One group of six children is seated around the teacher. She is teaching a lesson on place value and regrouping, or carrying.

The teacher sits on a small chair, the children on the floor around her. In the middle of the floor the teacher has marked the following pattern with masking tape:

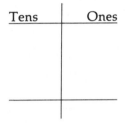

Nearby is a basket of blocks, the kind that can be attached to one another. The teacher says, "Show me how we make fourteen." A child places ten blocks in the "Tens" column and four blocks in the "Ones" column. The teacher has the child click the ten blocks together. On the floor, the pattern now looks like this:

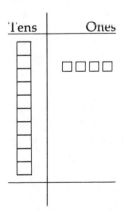

The teacher says, "What happens if we add five more?" A child places five more blocks in the "Ones" column. The pattern is as follows:

"How many ones do we have now?" asks the teacher.

"Nine," says a child.

"Let's check," says the teacher. They count the nine blocks in the "Ones" column. "How many do we have altogether?" asks the teacher.

"Nineteen," says a child.

"Let's write it down," says the teacher. On a portable slate she writes:

Tens	Ones
1	4
	5
1	9

"What's going to happen when you have more than ten ones?" she asks. She has the children place the fourteen blocks on the floor pattern again, and this time asks them to add nine ones. The pattern now looks like this:

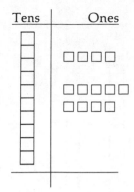

"Can we leave all the ones there?" she asks.

A child says, "No, because you can make a ten." The teacher has the child "make a ten" in the "Ones" column by clicking ten blocks together. The pattern now looks like this:

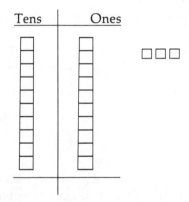

The teacher says, "Now carry the new ten over to the 'Tens' column." A child picks up the new stack of ten blocks and literally carries it over to the "Tens" column. The pattern now looks like this:

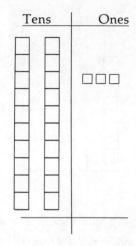

The teacher asks, "Now how many tens do we have?"

"Two," says a child.

"How many do we have altogether?"

"Twenty-three."

"Let's write it down," says the teacher. On the slate she writes:

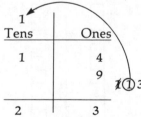

"That's carrying," she says. The lesson continues, the teacher asking the children to add different combinations of blocks requiring regrouping and to help her write down what they have done afterward.

THE USE OF CALCULATORS

Pocket calculators have become so inexpensive and so popular that before long virtually every schoolchild will have access to one. Their presence in school raises important questions about the nature of instruction in mathematics.

Calculators enable children to solve accurately and quickly computational problems that might otherwise pose great difficulty. And certainly in the outside world of business and everyday living, they are in widespread use. Some teachers and scholars therefore suggest that schools should spend less time on drill and practice in computation and more time on problem solving, estimation, and the checking and interpretation of results.

On the other hand, some people worry that the use of calculators will keep children from learning necessary lifelong computational skills. They urge schools to forbid their use until the basic skills have been mastered.

In the authors' view, the content and emphasis of the mathematics curriculum will change greatly in the age of calculators and computers—and no doubt the change will involve a shift away from some forms of computation (like multiplication or long division problems involving numbers with three or more digits) toward the use of computation in problem solving and toward other mathematical topics. For the immediate future, however, the math curriculum in most schools has not yet been changed by calculators, and the trick is to use the calculator as an aid to mastering fundamental computational skills.

Good teachers have children use calculators to

- Assist in learning number facts. The child enters a problem like 9×5. He gives the answer, then presses the $=$ sign to get the correct answer and check his own response.
- Check accuracy. The child solves a problem or completes an

exercise without using the calculator. He then repeats it on the calculator to check his own work.

Good teachers also have children check the calculator for the reasonableness of its answers. Children should not accept the calculator's every response as correct—perhaps the wrong number was entered, or entered in the wrong order, or the wrong function key was pressed. Children should estimate the answer to a problem and use their common sense if a computer's response seems wide of the mark.

WHAT TO LOOK FOR IN A GOOD SECOND-GRADE MATHEMATICS PROGRAM

Like first graders, most second graders enjoy their work in mathematics and continue to learn number ideas and facts quickly. The good program continues to be one that stimulates the child's thinking, tickles his curiosity, and challenges him to use his mind. If the answers to most or all of the following questions are yes, chances are your child is participating in an effective program. If many answers are no, you may want to inquire further by talking with your child's teacher and, possibly, the principal.

What to Look for in the Classroom

When you visit your child's classroom, do you see

- Number lines displayed on the walls or on the floor?
- Graphs of many kinds on many subjects, reflecting work that the teacher and the class have done?

- Chips, counters, Cuisenaire rods, and similar objects used for counting and sorting?
- Rulers, scales, thermometers, and other measuring devices?
- Pictures of two-dimensional shapes and three-dimensional objects used for exploring geometric properties?
- Worksheets done by children showing good work that they have done?

What to Look for From the Teacher

Does your child's second-grade teacher

- Describe clearly what the class has been doing in mathematics and what she plans for it to do?
- Provide time each day, or at least on most days, for mathematical activity?
- Provide time and opportunity for the children to learn and practice using number facts?
- Provide time and opportunity for the children to understand the mathematical ideas and relationships they are learning?
- Use concrete objects to help children understand mathematical ideas?
- Know your child's individual abilities and feelings about mathematics?
- Show enthusiasm about teaching mathematics?

What to Look for From Your Child

In the course of the second-grade year, does your child

- Seem interested in numbers, quantities, and mathematical relationships?
- Show a sense of excitement and confidence in using his mind for math?

- Describe math activities he has done in class?
- Bring home papers or worksheets reflecting work that he has done?
- Seem able to do the work listed in "The Signs of Progress"?

HOW TO HELP YOUR CHILD AT HOME

In the second grade most children still want to please their teacher. They feel good about what they do in school, and they resist suggestions that things should be done differently. ("That's not the way *we* do it"). Because your child's progress depends upon his confidence in the teacher, you should beware of voicing criticism or of working at cross-purposes with her. However, after consulting with the teacher, there are things you can do at home to reinforce what your child is learning at school.

Do's

- Talk to your child's teacher to learn about your child's math program and to ask what you can do at home.
- Praise and encourage your child's efforts to "use mathematics": to count, to estimate, to measure, to use numbers.
- Continue to estimate and measure with your child. Before you build things or move furniture or dig the garden, have your child help you measure the objects and area involved. Record the measurements, and discuss them together.
- Ask the teacher what kinds of mistakes your child makes in arithmetic. Find old workbooks containing similar problems, and help your child with them. Do easy problems first, to build confidence.
- Help your child solve word problems. (See the section "Problem Solving" above.) Be sure that your child understands the

problem; have him state it in his own words. Be sure to estimate the answer in advance and to check it afterward.
- Help your child to use a calculator to assist in learning number facts and to check accuracy in computation.

Don'ts

- Don't be impatient. Your time with your child should be loving and supportive, not tense and anxiety-provoking.
- Don't persist with an activity if your child becomes frustrated or inattentive.
- Don't say that you (or some people) are just "no good at math." Almost everyone can learn second-grade mathematics. Don't promote a defeatist attitude.
- Don't suggest that girls aren't as good in math as boys.

THE SIGNS OF PROGRESS

By the time they leave the second grade, children who are making normal progress in mathematics should have mastered most of the curriculum described above. They should be able to do the following.

Numbers and Numeration

- Count, read, and write the cardinal numbers from 1 to 1,000. Count forward and backward by ones, twos, threes, fours, and fives on a number line.
- Recognize fractions with numerators of 1–9 and denominators of 1–99.
- Recognize money notation to $100.

- Understand the meaning of each digit in three-digit numbers (hundreds, tens, ones).
- Understand the meaning of zero in the place-value system.

Operations With Whole Numbers

- Demonstrate knowledge of addition and subtraction facts through 18.
- Add and subtract two- and three-digit numbers that do not require regrouping (carrying or borrowing).
- Add and subtract two-digit numbers that do require regrouping.
- Understand multiplication as repeated addition.
- Demonstrate knowledge of multiplication facts through 25.
- Understand division as repeated subtraction and as the number of equivalent subsets of a given set.
- Demonstrate knowledge of division facts through 25.
- Use arithmetic knowledge and skill to solve simple word problems.

Operations With Fractions

- Divide whole objects into equal parts and relate part to whole (½, ⅓, ¼, ⅕, ⅙, ⅛, ⅒).
- Divide sets of objects into equal parts and relate part to whole (½, ⅓, ¼, ⅕, ⅙, ⅛, ⅒).
- Locate halves on a number line and on a ruler.

Probability and Statistics

- Collect, organize, and record information using two or more categories at a time. Arrange data in tables and graphs.
- Tally the information obtained by data gathering and graphing.

Compare the amounts in each category in terms of number, equality, and inequality.

Geometry and Measurement

- Make rough estimates and comparisons of size, distance, weight, capacity, temperature, time.
- Measure lengths in inches, feet, yards; centimeters, decimeters, meters.
- Measure weight in ounces, pounds; grams, kilograms.
- Measure capacity in ounces, pints, quarts; deciliters, liters.
- Tell time to the year, month, week, day, hour, minute, second.
- Read both the Fahrenheit and Celsius thermometers.

Most children acquire these skills by the end of the second grade. If by the middle of the second-grade year your child does not seem to be making normal progress, you should talk with his teacher. Perhaps he is simply developing more slowly than some; perhaps the class is "behind" where the teacher wishes it to be and will catch up soon; or perhaps your child has a learning problem that needs attention. Explore each of these possibilities with the teacher and hear her out before jumping to your own conclusions.

Some children progress more rapidly than others. If your child shows unusual proficiency, you may wish to talk to the teacher to see what adjustments, if any, should be made in his program and to obtain suggestions about how you can enrich his experience at home.

Writing in the Second Grade

There has been a great deal of interest in the teaching of writing in recent years. The way the writer goes about writing has been the subject of study in education departments in universities all around the nation. Teachers have joined together to study the best ways to teach writing. Many books have been written about writing for lay people and for teachers. The consensus of professional educators is that there is a specific process involved in writing and that this process can be taught to children.

Experts who have studied writing have assigned certain names to the steps that writers follow in their creative endeavor. We should all remember that these are simply names that are used to describe the writing process. They have no intrinsic value in themselves; the point is to follow the steps, not to use the words. All writers do not write in the same way, but there are certain generalizations one can make about the writing process that can help teachers help children.

THE WRITING PROCESS

The writer always thinks about what he is planning to write. He may talk to others about his ideas or he may not. He may do research on his subject, make lists, make outlines, or make formal written observations. This step is sometimes called *rehearsal*, or *prewriting*.

The next step is for some the most difficult. It is the rough attempt to organize thoughts on paper. This stage of the process, *drafting*, is similar to the artist's first sketches. At this point the writer is most concerned with the content of his essay, his story, his poem. He may compose by hand, on the typewriter, or on the word processor. He is not overly concerned with his spelling or handwriting or typing at this point. The product of this step is usually called the *first draft*, or *rough draft*.

Some writers revise and edit their work before they show it to an editor. Many, particularly beginning writers, show their rough drafts to a friend or to members of a writers' workshop. They try their work out on an audience and hope to get useful feedback. A helpful audience will say, for example, "I'd like to know more about. . . ," "I wish you would tell me more how the soup smelled," or "When the man was walking, did he limp or did he tiptoe?"

Negative comments, such as "Your story is too short" or "Your spelling is terrible," are not helpful. They would discourage any writer and provide no suggestions on how to improve the written piece. The writer listens to the comments, selects the ones that seem to be right, and *revises* his work. He may rearrange paragraphs, add some paragraphs, get rid of others. He may add details or he may delete some if he has been exhaustive in his description. He then *edits* his work, checking the spelling, punctuation, grammar, and usage. When his work is as correct as he can make it, he recopies it, types it on the typewriter or word processor, or asks someone else to do so.

THE SECOND-GRADE WRITER

The second-grade classroom is a writers' workshop. Children's writing should be displayed everywhere. Some classrooms have it hanging from strings stretched across the classroom. One teacher has a large poster called "Writers' Workshop Questions," which asks

- What happened?
- When did it happen?
- Where did it happen?
- How did it happen?
- Who was there?
- How did you feel?
- How would we know?
- Add details: What kind? What color? How did it move? How did it sound?
- Do you have an interesting lead?
- Do you have a satisfying ending?
- Do you have a strong title?

In another classroom writing is posted on a large bulletin board outside the room for passersby to see. One child has written her story on a snowman cut from construction paper. It reads:

Once there was a snowman. His name was Ben. He lived in Snowland. He had a black hat and eyes made of sticks. He was made out of snow. He only had two friends, the little girl and the rabbit. The snowman lived in a house.

There is no typical second-grade writer, although most children still choose topics from their personal lives. The stories range from simple picture labeling to highly focused, well-organized writing. Many second-grade writers are fluent, keeping long accounts of incidents and feelings in private journals. Children in the second grade are becoming aware of the concept of audience. Previously their writing has been for themselves rather than others. With the awareness of audience comes worry— worry that their stories won't be good enough, that the other children may not like them. The choice of a topic becomes more important.

Unlike the first grader, who uses drawing as a way to focus on a subject, the second grader uses talk or conversation during the rehearsal, or prewriting, stage. Talking helps him choose his topic and set up a framework for it. He may speak to the teacher or to a classmate. The teacher demonstrates to the class how to conduct an interview; she may interview a child in front of a small group so that the others will learn by imitation.

Once he has selected his topic and decided what he wishes to include, the child is ready to make the rough draft. Typical of second-grade writing are long chronological narrative accounts, called *bed-to-bed* stories by writing teachers, and *all-about* pieces, which catalog information. Some second-grade pieces could be titled "All About My New Brother," "All About My Vacation," or "All About My Garden." Second-grade children depend on words like *then* and *and* as conjunctions. Sentence structure is usually simple, following a basic pattern. Some children still use illustrations, but many do not. Handwriting is not a major task for most second graders. A few still find it so. The teacher, a volunteer, or an aide should allow the child who has trouble to dictate so that he may write his story.

Revision becomes an important part of the writing process in second grade. After the drafting process is over, the second-grade writer is ready to try his work out on an audience. Some classrooms have an "author's chair," a special seat for the child who is reading his work to the group. The audience may be his teacher, another pupil, or a group of his peers. Good teachers act as role models, showing the audience how to be skillful and helpful critics. The audience's job is to help the author improve his piece. The second-grade author is vulnerable to negative criticism. Perhaps we all are. Teachers of adult writing classes say that positive, helpful interest and good suggestions are more productive strategies and yield better results than negative comments.

After hearing the audience's comments, the second-grade author revises. He adds, deletes, reorganizes, and fleshes out. He cuts his work with scissors, staples, Scotch-tapes, crosses out, and writes between the lines. These techniques enable him to concentrate his efforts on revising rather than recopying.

Most second graders can edit their work by themselves after a conference with the teacher. After editing, he makes the final copy by hand or on the typewriter or word processor. Figure 1 is an example of an edited final draft of second-grade writing.

Writing is an important part of the second-grade curriculum and should be encouraged. Some classrooms have a corner of their room devoted to a library of work by classroom authors. Children may take books out and read their friends' stories. Some schools have a parent group that publishes books. Trained volunteers act as editors with children, discussing titles, pagination, and dedications. They type the books and submit them to the principal, who places a publishing seal on them.

SPELLING AND HANDWRITING IN THE SECOND GRADE

Although spelling improves in the second grade, many children still use phonetic spelling. In most classrooms, there is a spelling curriculum in the second grade. Many teachers use spelling books with prepared spelling lists. Others make their own lists, including words from children's writing and classroom units of study, and words related to seasons of the year or holidays. If

Tracks!

Jordan
Milman

Tracks in the snow
Perhaps made by a shovel
Look like little cliffs
As if I were looking down
from too many miles up to
Say,
and when I look the other
way
Without my Imagination
It just looks like trees
with snow.
By jordan milman

Figure 1

homework is assigned in second grade, spelling is often the subject. Children are asked to write words several times, make up sentences, or compose stories using the words. Teachers talk with the children about the words in class, so that the good spelling lesson is often a vocabulary lesson as well.

Improvement in spelling is probably more the result of reading and seeing the same words over and over than of a formal spelling program. Nevertheless, spelling lessons do help, and the more children see and write words spelled correctly, the more they will spell them correctly themselves. Some children will find spelling easy and some will have difficulty with it all their lives. Even though your child may have difficulty now, remember that he will improve and he will also learn to use a dictionary. There are a few learning-disabled children who will always have serious trouble with spelling. Second grade is very early to make that judgment. However, if you think your child has unusual trouble spelling correctly and you are worried, speak to your child's teacher.

For most children, handwriting becomes a little easier in second grade. Legibility remains the goal of a handwriting program. Although a beautiful hand is always admired, it is not a priority in today's schools. It is, however, important to have a handwriting that is readable. Most classrooms have a handwriting workbook for children in which to practice after the teacher has demonstrated a writing lesson on the blackboard. Some children will find handwriting to be an easily learned skill. Others will find it an unpleasant but necessary task. For a few, it will always be an arduous task. Word processors and typewriters will offer a welcome aid to those few. If you think handwriting is particularly difficult for your child and it is causing a problem with the rest of his schoolwork, by all means, contact his teacher.

A GOOD WRITING PROGRAM

A good writing program is one that

- Understands that children's experience and their perception of it is an important topic for writing.
- Helps children to be good observers, to listen to sounds, to notice smell, to see detail.
- Shows children how to incorporate the detail they observe in their writing.
- Provides a writing center, a place where there are pencils and blank stapled books, a place where children may go if they wish to write.
- Provides time for the entire writing process, as well as time for children to listen to and read their classmates' writing.
- Teaches children how to be good editors, to ask the right questions, to be specific, to be positive and encouraging and yet helpful, to be committed to helping each author produce a better piece.
- Recognizes the difference between handwriting and writing, helping children whose handwriting is an overwhelming task by allowing them to dictate occasional stories or use a word processor.
- Values literature, encourages children to read, provides time for reading aloud to them.
- Recognizes that writing, like speaking, is a trial-and-error skill and needs encouragement and nurturing.
- Displays children's writing prominently and attractively.
- Stresses the specifics of what is good about some writing samples.
- Shows interest in every child's writing.

Interest is perhaps the highest compliment a reader can pay to an author. Empty compliments are not helpful. Nor is gratuitous criticism. What is helpful are questions about the content of the piece, questions that ask for more information. A teacher might say to a child about his writing, "You really interested me with your story. Tell me . . ."

What You Can Do

You can help your child in a variety of ways. You can

- Act as a role model by writing yourself, writing letters, and so on. Don't speak of writing as if it were an onerous task.
- Tell your child stories and encourage him to tell you stories.
- Help your child be a good observer. Talk about what both of you see, hear, and smell.
- Provide him with a well-lit place to write and ample paper and pencil.
- Display your child's art and writing prominently in your home.
- Spell a word for him if he asks you while he is writing.
- Show interest in the stories he tells and writes.
- Encourage him to write at home. Have him write letters and make greeting cards for friends and family members.
- Applaud his writing efforts. Remember, he is just at the beginning of his writing career.

A positive word goes a long way. Commenting on what is wrong is easy to do, but only discourages. Your child will want to write more if you mention what you like about his writing and show enthusiasm for it. Remember that your child is a second grader, not an adult. His spelling, punctuation, and handwriting will improve with time, practice, and instruction. So will his writing if you and the teacher offer warm encouragement.

Social Studies in the Second Grade

In the kindergarten and the first grade, children's instruction in the social studies—those studies of humankind we in adult life call history, geography, economics, anthropology, sociology, political science, and so on—is likely to be an incidental outgrowth of learning appropriate classroom behavior and talking about families and holidays. By the time children enter the second grade, however, instruction typically becomes much more direct. Whatever the content of the program, children read books related to social studies, paint pictures, sing songs, write stories or "reports." Teachers may plan and teach lessons with an explicit social studies focus. The work tends to be integrated with other subjects, like reading or literature, and reading, writing, and arithmetic still consume the bulk of classroom time. However, social studies has come to occupy an important place in the school curriculum.

At the same time, across the country there is no consensus about what a good second-grade social studies program should contain. (Many social studies textbooks widely used at this level emphasize the study of the local community, but others deal with "The World Around Us" or "Places Far and Near." Many schools use no texts at all.) Some programs emphasize our national traditions; others focus on the interrelatedness of all people. You should not be surprised or upset if the content of your child's social studies program is different from another child's in another classroom. What matters is that your child's knowledge of the world continue to expand and that he acquire skills and attitudes that make additional learning both possible and likely.

THE SECOND-GRADE SOCIAL STUDIES CURRICULUM

Among the ideas (concepts) commonly taught in the second-grade social studies curriculum are the following:

Community

- People live in communities to meet their needs, to get help, to have companionship.
- People live in rural, urban, and suburban communities; each has similarities and differences.
- Communities develop rules and laws to govern and protect community members.
- People in communities sometimes disagree about rules, rights, and responsibilities.
- People in all communities have common needs—food, shelter, clothing, health, safety.
- People in all communities produce goods and services that are useful to others.
- People in all communities consume goods and services.
- By producing goods and services, people earn the money to buy the things they need or want.
- Communities collect taxes to provide services for the good of all people—fire department, police department, school system, and so on.

- The nature of a community depends in part upon its geographic environment.
- The nature of a community depends in part upon its traditions.
- Communities change as time passes and circumstances change.

Nation

- Our nation is a democracy, a "free country" in which "all men are created equal."
- The nation provides services that communities could not on their own.
- People in our nation celebrate certain national holidays, such as Martin Luther King Day, Lincoln's Birthday, Washington's Birthday, Memorial Day, the Fourth of July, which honor our traditions.
- Our nation has people who make and carry out the laws—Congress, the courts, the president.
- Our nation changes as time passes and circumstances change.

In addition to participating in experiences that develop these ideas, children acquire certain skills that remain important throughout school: working cooperatively with others, finding and reporting relevant information, classifying data, using simple maps and globes. Although these skills are important, they are usually less specifically and systematically defined than those in reading or mathematics tend to be.

TEACHING THE SECOND-GRADE SOCIAL STUDIES CURRICULUM

In the second grade, as in the first, much of the teaching and learning of social studies is relatively informal—discussions of current events, trips to nearby places of interest, celebration of holidays. Some of it becomes increasingly direct; many schools have a social studies curriculum that teachers must teach, and textbooks are used more often. Most teachers relate topics in social studies to literature, art, music, and, sometimes, science.

The following scene from one second-grade classroom demonstrates a social studies lesson.

Mid-January. The class has been studying the life of Martin Luther King, Jr.—his holiday is approaching. They have read stories about him, looked at pictures, listened to his speeches on records, watched a film of the 1963 peace march, heard the crowds applauding and cheering. On the wall is a poem by Langston Hughes ("Hold Fast to Dreams"). The teacher has assigned each child a separate event or period in King's life, and the children have been reading about them and preparing short written reports.

Today the class is working together, writing a group poem. The teacher stands near a large pad on an easel, writing down what the children say. She asks them questions about King, and writes down the words and phrases they use when they answer. She reminds them of the crowds, of the sounds, of the way he spoke. They use their own words to capture the feeling. When the page is almost full, the teacher cuts it up and gives words and phrases to groups of three children. Each group is to arrange the words and phrases as it wishes, and to add one new line. As they work, the teacher explains, with a child's help, what a *refrain* is. She asks what a good refrain would be for their poem. A child chooses the line, "Changed the law to make us brothers." She asks the class if they like that line. They say they do, and she writes it down.

After a while she collects what the groups have written and arranges the pieces on the big pad (with the help of the children). She edits a bit, changing the spelling and omitting some words. Here is the result:

In Memory—Martin Luther King, Jr.

Powerfully he spoke to all
Thoughtful, kind and good
He wanted things to be as they should.
    Changed the laws to make us brothers.

He spoke for peace
His voice made fiery words
"My people, I have dreams for you
I hope one day they'll all come true.
Someday, I know someone will get me
But I am ready!"
    Changed the laws to make us brothers.

His thundering words so strong
How mightily he came along
"Fight with your mouths
and not your fists!"
Too bad he's not around
He will be missed.
    Changed the laws to make us brothers.

The Nobel Prize he shared with all
For nonviolence was his aim
He was murdered—what a shame.
His dream is still alive!
    Changed the laws to make us brothers.

In the next few days the children will illustrate the poem, and it will be beautifully displayed on the wall. On the Friday before Martin Luther King Day, the parents will be invited to attend a celebration at which the children will read their reports, sing songs ("We Shall Overcome"), and perform a skit the teacher and children have written.

WHAT TO LOOK FOR IN A GOOD SECOND-GRADE SOCIAL STUDIES PROGRAM

As in the first grade, the specific content of the second-grade social studies program is not important. What matters is that the teacher nourish your child's curiosity about the world and that your child's knowledge and understanding of our country's traditions and how other people in the world work and live continue to grow. Here are some signs of progress to look for:

- Does your child show curiosity about other people, other places, other times?
- Does your child seem aware of major current events? Does he say they talk about them in school?
- Does your child bring home stories or pictures that reflect social studies activity, such as materials relating to a current holiday?
- Does your child seem increasingly aware of where he is in space and time, relative to other people and the past?

If the answers to questions like these are yes, your child is making normal progress. If the answers are no, you may want to talk to your child's teacher and ask her what else the children will be doing before the end of the school year.

Science in the Second Grade

children guessed (but only a few
and down they forgot as up they grew
autumn winter spring summer) . . .

e.e. cummings knew what many others knew: that young children rush to explore their new world with keen intuition and joyful eagerness, but that this freshness fades as time passes. The task of the second-grade science program is to keep enthusiasm and curiosity alive while imparting the tools and habits of scientific inquiry. In the content and skills that it teaches, the second-grade science program is much like the first-grade science program, although it can make use of the reading and math skills that children have acquired in the first grade. The challenge for the second-grade teacher is to provide experiences that continue to stimulate children's curiosity and imagination even as they become accustomed to school routines and activity.

THE SECOND-GRADE SCIENCE CURRICULUM

In the decades prior to the 1960s, the emphasis of most elementary-school science programs was upon content (information). In the 1960s and 1970s, the focus changed to process (scientific method)—to *doing* science rather than learning about it. In the 1980s leading teachers and scholars agree that a good science program combines both content and process. They also agree that children should have experiences in the earth, life, and physical sciences, that the specific content of these experiences is unimportant provided they are taught well, and that these experiences can be integrated into other learning activities in reading, language development, and mathematics.

Good teachers at this level continue to involve children in activities that explore the properties of objects and the events in the natural world around them. They care for animals and observe what they eat, when they sleep, how they care for themselves, how they change as time passes. They plant seeds and watch them grow, noting the different effects of moisture, dryness, heat, cold, light, darkness. They handle wood, clay, stone, metal, plastic, and learn by "doing" that different materials have different properties—weight, color, texture, hardness, brightness, reflectivity, transparency. They watch what happens to solids and liquids when heat is applied and when it is removed; they experiment with what sinks and what floats in water, and try to guess why.

At the same time, children continue to develop the skills and attitudes of scientific inquiry. They observe closely, classify objects, properties, and events, make measurements, record and graph data. They interpret and describe what they experience and begin to question or refute previous findings as a result of new or conflicting information.

TEACHING THE SECOND-GRADE SCIENCE CURRICULUM

As in the first grade, the specific content of the science program varies widely in the second grade. There is no generally accepted science curriculum in use throughout the country at this level. Some schools and teachers use excellent units of instruction developed by such organizations as the Elementary Science Study (ESS) and the Science Curriculum Improvement Study (SCIS). Others follow state or local curricula, adapting the content and materials to local needs and resources. Always the better programs involve children directly in the activity. Children do not merely watch, listen, or read—they themselves handle and act upon the objects they are studying and observe the results of their own activity. Sometimes the experiences grow naturally out of some ongoing activity in which the class is involved, as when the children collect colored leaves on their fall trip to the post office and bring them back to the classroom for closer inspection and discussion. Sometimes they are more sustained units of instruction, at which children spend some time each day for a period of several days or weeks.

One class participated in such a unit on butterflies. The teacher found three caterpillars on a milkweed plant in a field near her home and brought them to class. She put them in a box with proper air and moisture, and the children fed them milkweed leaves and watched them grow. They used magnifying glasses to watch the caterpillars eat and walk. They counted the legs—answers varied—and drew pictures of them. They tried to measure the caterpillars' growth, using pieces of thread and rulers. Eventually first one and then the other caterpillars were found hanging upside down from a silken button underneath a leaf. The children examined the change—pupation—with amazement. The teacher had the children read and write stories and poems about butterflies, and several children helped build a large cage to hold the butterflies when they emerged. As the pupae developed, the children watched them darken, and they began to see signs of wings forming within the cases. Toward the end, the covering of the pupae gradually became transparent, and a sense of expectancy grew in the class.

In this case, the children were not present to watch the butterflies emerge—the school clock and nature's do not always coincide. But one morning when the children arrived, there were three monarch butterflies exercising their wings. For two days the children watched them closely, observing their reaction to light and feeding them sugar water. Some classes have watched butterflies mate, have collected their eggs, and have seen the life cycle start over again. In this class, however, the children felt that the butterflies should be set free. The teacher agreed, and one morning they released them into the warm May air, wishing them good luck. But the lesson of the miracle of life and change remained with the children.

WHAT TO LOOK FOR IN A GOOD SECOND-GRADE SCIENCE PROGRAM

A good second-grade science program involves children in activities that explore the properties of objects and events in the natural world around them and helps children develop skills of observation and classification that are fundamental to the scientific method. Here are some things you might look for:

- Does your child's teacher provide time for experiences in science?
- Are there plants, animals, and other such objects in the classroom?
- Does your child actually use—handle, weigh, measure, feed—these objects?

- Does some of your child's reading and writing relate to science?
- Is your child asked to use his powers of observation closely and is he challenged to use his mind about what he perceives?
- Does your child feel good about using his mind and senses to explore new experiences?

THE PRIMARY
YEARS

The Arts in the Primary Years

Let's begin with this: the arts are not a frill. The arts are, or ought to be, as fundamental and as basic to a well-rounded full education as reading and writing. Our educational tradition has ruptured the connection between imagination and intellect; but in real life as we live it, thinking and feeling and imagining are fused. As Ernest Boyer, president of the Carnegie Foundation for the Advancement of Teaching, has said: "Now more than ever, all people need to see clearly, hear acutely and feel sensitively through the arts. These languages are no longer simply desirable but are essential if we are to convey adequately our deepest feelings, and survive with civility and joy."

The Council for Basic Education, among others, agrees that the "study of the arts is basic." Not only does such study help children learn the basic skills of looking, listening, reading, writing, and computing, but it is important in its own right, helping children perceive and create images that communicate directly through the senses. (Think of how powerful these images are in our television-addicted society!)

Unfortunately, in many schools today tightened budgets and a narrow back-to-basics attitude have limited the attention paid to this part of education. As a concerned parent, you should encourage your school system not to neglect this important aspect of your child's education.

ACTIVITIES IN THE ARTS

Most American schools divide the arts into "Art" (drawing, painting, sculpting, collage-making, weaving, woodworking) and "Music" (singing, dancing, playing instruments, listening to music). Good teachers relate these activities to one another and to other subjects in the curriculum—literature, history, science—as well as to holidays or special events.

Children in the primary years love these activities. As *Coming to Our Senses*, a report of the Special Project Panel of the American Council for the Arts in Education (New York, McGraw Hill, 1977), said: "The arts are the natural work of children. The arts are like play—creative, exploratory, purposeful—reality confirming. When painting and constructing, moving and dancing, singing and playing instruments, making and performing plays and stories and poems and songs—when all these are woven into the whole school day, basic subjects are learned more quickly—and are unforgettable."

A good art program in the primary years encourages children to express their ideas and feelings in a wide variety of forms and with a wide variety of materials. Children experiment with oil paints, crayons, clay, watercolors, fingerpaints, sand, sawdust, Play-Doh, string, thread, papier-mâché, colored paper, and a wide variety of found materials, like boxes, buttons, bottle tops, coat hangers, spools, pipe cleaners, shoe laces, egg crates, and scraps of cloth. They use brushes, sponges, scissors, paste, pencils, chalk, glue. They make drawings, paintings, murals, mobiles, collages, displays. They discover how these tools and materials work, alone and in combination. Sometimes they make art to reflect what they have done or read—they return from a trip to the park in the spring and paint the early-flowering trees. Sometimes they make art first and then write about it—they draw a picture showing how they help at home and then write a story to explain the picture. Sometimes they make art for the sheer joy of doing so. Kindergarten children especially are often more involved in the process of making things than in the created product. But the good teacher saves what they have done and displays it for all to see.

Throughout these years children become increasingly comfortable with the art mediums and techniques. Typically, their work becomes less sketchy and somewhat more realistic. This is still not the age for realism, however, and good teachers encourage children to express things as they see and feel them. A purple cow is not unrealistic if the cow is sad and if purple is a sad color for the child. The goal is to stimulate children's creativity and give them the means to express it freely. Coloring within the lines may encourage neatness, but it is the antithesis of a good art program.

ACTIVITIES IN MUSIC

In much the same way, a good music program in the primary years introduces children to a wide variety of forms of musical expression and encourages them to express themselves in these forms. Children sing, march, dance, and move to rhythm, clapping, swaying, stomping, skipping, swinging arms. They experiment with fast and slow, high and low, loud and soft, long and short. Sometimes the teacher may play records. Sometimes she plays the piano or the guitar, and the children sing with her. Sometimes the class sings without accompaniment. Sometimes the children make up a dance to match the mood of a story or a painting; sometimes they paint or write to reflect the feeling of a song. Sometimes they make music on their own instruments— rhythm sticks, wooden rattles, soda cans with marbles or pebbles in them, triangles, tambourines, chimes, glasses filled with water. Sometimes they sing songs they have learned because they like them—"Frère Jacques," "The Farmer in the Dell"—and sometimes they make up their own songs, to tell a story or express an emotion. Sometimes they sing to entertain an audience—their parents or another class. But most of the time they sing to please themselves.

At this age there is little drill and little attention to musical notation or other formal matters. The goal is to help children enjoy themselves through music, to be comfortable with it, to become increasingly discerning as they listen to it and proficient as they perform. A wonderful Welsh teacher whom we knew once said that in a happy school you should hear children singing more often than you should hear the clock tick. No doubt there are schools where one hears neither, but wouldn't our schools seem happier places if the air were more often filled with children's song?

Computers in the Primary Years

In recent years the number of microcomputers in American elementary-school classrooms has grown dramatically. A decade ago there were virtually none. In 1981 the National Center for Educational Statistics reported that more than half the schools in the country owned at least one computer. Since then the numbers have continued to multiply. The price of hardware has dropped, software has become more available, and a bandwagon effect has taken hold. Today, computers are as frequently seen in rural schools and in the inner cities as they are in the nation's affluent suburbs. They are to classrooms today as television sets were to American households in the 1950s and 1960s—recently arrived, ubiquitous, and here to stay.

Despite the rapid growth in numbers, there is as yet no generally accepted pattern of use. Most educators agree that children should acquire "computer literacy" but few agree on what it is. Some educators believe that computers should be used to reinforce what is taught in the traditional curriculum, for example, to provide drill and practice in number facts or to serve as an editing tool in the writing process. Some believe that children should study the computer itself: they should learn how it works, how to program it, how to use it to solve problems. Some believe that most children need only know how to use the software packages that have become increasingly available, and that children should use such software in the study of math, science, social studies, and other subjects.

Still other educators believe that computer technology will soon make the traditional curriculum obsolete. For them, the computer is as revolutionary as the printing press was once, as much an extension of the power of the human mind as the lever is of the human body. They would allow the child to interact with the computer and, under guidance, create in part his own curriculum. One leading spokesman for this view is Seymour Papert, the Massachusetts Institute of Technology professor who developed the programming language Logo. In Papert's vision, "The child programs the computer and, in doing so, both acquires a sense of mastery over a piece of the most modern and powerful technology and establishes an intimate contact with some of the deepest ideas from science, from mathematics, and from the art of intellectual model building."

THE USE OF THE COMPUTER IN INSTRUCTION

Professor Robert Taylor of Teachers College, Columbia University, identifies three chief uses of the computer in schools: as a tool, as a tutor, and as a tutee.

The computer may be used as a *tool* to calculate, to draw, or to write. One important example of such use is word processing. Children of primary-school age can learn to type their "stories" on the computer (the skill is called *keyboarding*) and to use the word-processing program to edit their own work—to insert or delete words, to change the order of the text, to check spelling. Many teachers claim that children who use this technique are more highly motivated to write, that they learn the steps of the writing process more quickly, and that their writing is of better quality.

The computer may be used as a *tutor* to teach or reinforce information or skills. For example, the computer may be programmed to teach children to count and to do simple addition and subtraction. The computer poses a question and the child types his answer. If the answer is correct, the program proceeds; if not, the program leads the child through a series of steps until the answer is correct. Some children are comfortable with this technique because the computer is infinitely patient and because no one sees their mistakes. They can proceed at their own pace, correcting themselves as they go, until they get everything right. Where such drill and practice is appropriate, this use of the computer (sometimes called *computer-assisted instruction*) can be very helpful. However, if the computer is used only in this way, much of its potential is wasted.

The computer is used as a *tutee* when the child programs it himself in order to accomplish a purpose. In this way the child not only learns programming skills (with their qualities of logic, precision, and economy), but acquires a deeper understanding of the subject he is writing the program about. The most common example of this use of the computer in primary classrooms today is the work children do with Logo. The child wishes to draw a house on the computer screen. To do so, he must write a computer program that will move the "turtle" (a triangular shape on the screen) in the desired directions for the desired distances. In doing so, he learns about programming—analyzing a task, sequencing, developing subroutines. He also learns about geometry—angles, squares, triangles, for example—and about the relationships between numbers and space. In contrast to computer-assisted instruction, in which someone else has developed the program and the answers are either right or wrong, in Logo the child is the programmer and learns through open-ended inquiry.

THE "WRITING TO READ" PROGRAM

The computer can also be used in ways that combine elements of these three approaches. In recent years software packages have been developed offering children interesting tools to use in pursuing their own learning. One noted example is the "Writing to Read" program developed by the educator John Henry Martin and the IBM Corporation. This program combines the computer (equipped with voice output and color graphics) with typewriters, audiocassettes, and tape recorders to help young children acquire reading readiness skills. Children write what they say and think and learn to read what they have written. Preliminary studies have shown this approach to be effective.

WHAT TO LOOK FOR IN YOUR SCHOOL

This pattern of widely varying uses of the computer is likely to continue for some time. Schools have not yet had time to adapt to the new technology. Much more thinking and experimentation needs to be done about the role of the computer in instruction. Despite the relatively high volume of computer sales, computers need to become accessible to more children more of the time. Better software needs to be developed. Teachers trained in the pre-computer era need to be reeducated, or gradually to give way to a younger generation, more at home with the computer.

Meanwhile, the technology itself will continue changing. A recent advertisement announced: "In the not-distant future one video disk will hold an entire Encyclopedia Britannica, including color photographs; disks occupying the same space as a typical teen's record collection will store the information necessary for a four-year college education." Who knows what other marvels lie beyond a layman's imagination? And how long will it take the schools to take advantage of the possibilities such marvels will present?

For the time being, you should not be too concerned about what your child is or is not doing with computers in school in the primary years. In most primary programs, computers are used marginally, if at all. If your school does have computers, you may want to find out what it is doing with them. You may also want to ask what use is made of computers in the upper grades.

But the best way you can help your child prepare for life in the computer age is to help him become comfortable with computers. If you have a computer at home, buy software that is appropriate for him and let him use—even "play"—with the machine. If you do not own one, show him computers in stores and office buildings, or let him use one at the public library. Treat them as a commonplace convenience, not a mystery. No doubt by the time your child is in high school, today's computers will seem old-fashioned. But his experience should make him as comfortable with computer technology as his parents were with television and his grandparents with the radio.

Health and Physical Education in the Primary Years

Most primary schools throughout the country have programs in health and physical education. In some states, they are required by law. Although you may not regard these programs as vital as learning to read and to do mathematics, they can be a very important part of your child's total development as a healthy, active human being.

HEALTH EDUCATION

Health education should not be confused with health services, concerned with physical examinations, inoculations, school safety, school cleanliness, first aid, and the like, and usually provided by the school nurse or physician. Health education attempts to instill knowledge, attitudes, and habits on such matters as

- Physical health, including rest and exercise, personal hygiene, nutrition, dental care, and substance abuse (tobacco, alcohol, other drugs).
- Mental health, including understanding of self, awareness of

feelings, respect for others, and decision-making (understanding of the consequences of one's actions).
- Safety, including crossing the street, talking to strangers, and care about what goes in the mouth.
- Sexuality, including parents and babies, and "my body belongs to myself."

Health education programs are usually conducted by the regular classroom teacher, although the nurse or another special teacher may sometimes be involved. In the primary years the emphasis is on developing healthy attitudes and habits, and most of the teaching is informal, a natural outgrowth of classroom routines or activities in social studies or science. For example, the teacher and the children wash their hands before snack time and eat good nutritional foods, such as apples, oranges, carrots, and graham crackers instead of high-sugar cookies. They look both ways before crossing the street, and they talk about families and babies when the eggs hatch and the chicks are born in the classroom.

Sometimes teachers do teach direct lessons about health. In one class the children were taught to classify foods according to their source—plant, animal, or man-made (candy, mustard, potato chips). They brought colored pictures of foods from magazines to class and tacked them on the bulletin board under the appropriate heading. They made a food-record booklet, in which they drew or pasted pictures of all they could remember about what they ate and drank (except water) for two days. They then discussed what they ate, using information supplied by the teacher about the nutrients in various foods. (The comparison between a soft drink and a glass of skim milk was startling!) After examining a few diets, they were asked to exchange some of their foods for more nutritious alternatives. The children made bar graphs of their own diets over a period of several weeks. The graphs were displayed on the wall, a constant reminder of who was eating in a healthy fashion.

PHYSICAL EDUCATION

Almost all schools provide some sort of physical education program, even if it consists of nothing more than letting children go outside to run around and let off steam. A good physical education program goes far beyond this simple activity, however. A well-conceived and well-taught program can help your child develop skills and habits that will stand him in good stead for a lifetime.

Partisans of physical education believe that physical fitness is a good thing in itself and that a child must be sound in body if he is to be sound in mind. They also believe that through individual and team games and activities, children can learn desirable attitudes and values of self-discipline, cooperation, and steadiness under pressure. Among the goals of the program are

- Physical fitness, including strength, endurance, agility, and vitality.
- Physical skills, including running, jumping, skipping, bending, and skills related to specific sports and activities.
- Desirable social values, including poise, self-respect, respect for others, cooperation, and sportsmanlike conduct.
- Recreational habits, including knowledge and skill at games to play with other children, and knowledge and skill at games to play throughout life.

Physical education programs in the primary years are usually taught by the classroom teacher, although some schools have physical education teachers, who meet with the class several times a week or even once a day. Among the most common activities are

- Games and sports, such as chasing games, relay games, and dodge ball.

- Rhythmic activities, such as dancing, pantomime, and creative movement.
- Self-testing and conditioning activities, such as skipping rope, tumbling, and balancing on a beam.

Good teachers provide a wide variety of activities and make sure that each child is involved, no matter what his physical ability.

Tests in the Primary Years

During your child's first three years in school he will probably be given one or more standardized tests. Schools typically administer such tests during the primary years to determine reading readiness, IQ, and achievement in the academic curriculum. The test results are not as important as they may be later in your child's schooling, but they do influence the way people think about your child. For this reason alone you should know what tests your child takes and have a reasonably clear idea of what the results do and do not mean.

STANDARDIZED TESTS

A standardized test is different from the classroom test or quiz the teacher gives to see how well her pupils are mastering the curriculum she is teaching. It is prepared by test specialists, produced by test publishers who are national in scope, contains explicit instructions for how it is to be given (timing, directions, for example), has machine-scored answer sheets, and has norms for interpreting the test results. The norms are based on the average performance of other children the same age who have taken the test. The test is "standardized" in the sense that it is taken under the same conditions and permits comparison of one score or a group of scores with a national sample. It measures a child's performance in comparison with the performance of other children the same age.

The standardized tests most commonly used in schools are of two types: achievement tests and aptitude tests.

Achievement Tests

Achievement tests measure how much a child has learned in a given subject. A reading achievement test, for example, measures a child's reading skills compared to those of other children his age in his class, his school, his state, and the country. Among the achievement tests in common use are the following:

California Achievement Tests
California Assessment Program Achievement Series
Comprehensive Tests of Basic Skills (CTBS)
Cooperative Primary Tests
Iowa Test of Basic Skills
Iowa Tests of Educational Development
Metropolitan Achievement Tests
Science Research Associates (SRA) Achievement Series
Stanford Achievement Series

Here is a typical question from a reading achievement test. The child reads this passage:

Mother and Bill did not know which way to drive. Mother looked at the map. She saw the right road. Then they knew where to go.

The child is then asked to check the right answer to a series of questions, such as the following:

Mother and Bill were going by
- [ ] plane
- [ ] train
- [ ] car
- [ ] ship

Aptitude Tests

Aptitude tests measure a child's ability to learn in specific subjects. They are not intended to measure what children have actually learned in class but to assess broad-scale abilities, such as verbal ability, memory, and reasoning ability, which the child needs in order to do schoolwork. Among the standardized aptitude tests in common use are the following:

California Test of Mental Maturity
Gates-MacGinitie Reading Skills Test
Lee-Clark Reading Readiness Test
Lorge-Thorndike Intelligence Tests
Metropolitan Readiness Test
Murphy Durrell Reading Readiness Analysis
Stanford-Binet IQ Test
Wechsler Preschool and Primary Scale of Intelligence
Wechsler Intelligence Scale for Children

IQ TESTS

One familiar form of aptitude test is the IQ (intelligence quotient) test. IQ tests measure basic mental abilities, such as verbal ability, memory, reasoning, and spatial perception. Children are given such tasks as sentence completions, word problems, and problems involving pictures and patterns. Here is a typical sentence completion problem:

The sun rises in the _____ and sets in the west.

A. summer   B. morning   C. east   D. end   E. sky

Although IQ tests are in disfavor among knowledgeable educators, they are still used in many schools. Supposedly, the IQ test can be used to predict how successful a child will be in school. And in a very broad way, it does. The problem is that often parents, teachers, and children themselves think that it means something it does not.

An IQ score is *not* a measure of a child's fixed innate capacity. All aptitude tests depend in part on what a child has already learned—the distinction between achievement and aptitude tests is not as absolute as it may seem. Research has shown that children can raise their IQ scores given proper instruction and encouragement.

Furthermore, intelligence itself is not a single attribute. There are many different mental abilities involved in the general trait we call intelligence. The magazine *Seventeen* has quoted Dr. Stephen Jay Gould, a famous Harvard professor and author of *The Mismeasure of Man*, as saying that "there's no such thing as a single measure of intelligence. You can't measure intelligence the way you can your foot size or your height."

The scores attained on IQ tests can also vary, depending on, for example, the conditions under which the child took the test or his energy level on that particular day. If you have reason to believe that your child's score is too low and if the school seems to think the matter is important, ask that your child be retested.

Finally, an IQ test cannot measure many of the traits we know to be important in determining success in school and in life—traits like common sense, motivation, responsibility, empathy, creativity, and insight.

TEST SCORES

The scores your child receives on standardized tests will probably be reported to you in one of the following forms: raw scores, percentiles, stanines, or grade equivalent scores.

Raw Scores

This is the number of questions your child answered correctly. A raw score doesn't tell you much. For example, what does "23" mean if you don't know how many questions there were in the test and how other children did, let alone what the test was about?

Percentiles

A percentile is *not* the percent of questions your child answered correctly. It indicates what percent of people in the norm group (others who took the test) your child scored above. For example, a score of 83 means that your child did better than 83 percent of the children in the norm group. (He may have answered only 70 percent of the questions correctly.)

Stanines

Stanines are a statistical measure that groups scores more broadly than percentiles. Stanines range from a low of 1 to a high of 9. Scores of 1, 2, and 3 are below average; 4, 5, and 6 average; 7, 8, and 9 above average.

Grade Equivalent Scores

Grade equivalent scores are reported as two digits separated by a decimal. The first digit stands for a grade in school, the second for a tenth of a year. A grade equivalent score of 2.5 means that the child scored as well on that test as an average child would in the fifth month of the second grade.

Grade equivalent scores are subject to a great deal of misunderstanding. For example, if your second-grade child scores 4.6 on a math test, it does *not* mean that your child should be doing fourth-grade math. The test may have contained no questions about topics normally covered in grades three and four. What the score means is that your child scored as well on the second-grade test as would an average child on the same test in the sixth month of fourth grade.

Similarly, if your second-grade child scores 1.4 on a reading test, it does *not* mean that your child should be back in first grade (although it may mean that your child should get special help). It means that your child scored as well on the second-grade test as would an average child in the fourth month of first grade.

Remember that a grade equivalent score is defined as a score that is in the middle for students at a grade level. Half the children in the nation are above and half are below—by definition. For these reasons you should be very wary when you hear of your child or someone else performing above or below grade level. Did you know that half the students at Harvard College are below average?

WHAT DO THE TESTS TELL US?

Schools use standardized tests to place and group children for instruction, to determine speed of instruction, to select appropriate learning tasks, to evaluate how well a school or class is achieving, and to determine what children are and are not learning. Such tests do tell us how one child's performance compares to that of others in the same grade, and they may help identify areas of strength and weakness. Because schools must have some way of standardizing the results of instruction from one classroom to another and because they need to provide measures of accountability to the public, standardized tests of some kind are a necessity.

But most standardized tests are too broadly gauged to tell you very much about your individual child. Almost any smart, competent classroom teacher can tell you more. For these reasons, you should resist any attempt to make decisions about your child based on test scores alone. Test scores are only one measure of your child's achievement and abilities, and an imperfect measure at that. Help your child to take the tests seriously, but do not overemphasize the results—to him, to the teacher, or to yourself.

The Gifted Child

New York State requires that all children who enter its public school system be screened to determine whether they are possibly handicapped or possibly gifted. The desk of one author contains a list of the possibly gifted in the school district that he serves. It is the "alpha" list of all children in the district, because the mission of the schools is to ascertain each child's gifts and talents and to nurture them appropriately.

Perhaps as children get older, this approach may be too broad to be effective. After all, there are children whose special gifts and talents set them apart from their peers and require special attention. But in the primary years, the authors believe, the needs of gifted and talented children can be well met by enriching the normal home and school situation. And the harm that may be done by labeling children too early—pushing some to do work for which they are not ready, writing others off because their developmental clock is more slowly paced—is an unnecessary evil.

THE SIGNS OF GIFTEDNESS

Many children are precocious; they may or may not be unusually gifted or talented. In particular, first children in a family or only children, who spend their early childhood years more with adults than with siblings or agemates, may seem more mentally advanced than other children of their age. How can you tell if you have a truly gifted child?

First of all, if you have a *truly* gifted child, you don't have to ask the question. No one had to test young Wolfgang Amadeus Mozart for giftedness. However, by the looser definition of the term in widespread use today, here are a few signs to look for in your young child:

- Speaking in complete sentences with relatively mature vocabulary at age 2–3.
- Reading signs, advertisements, books, and magazines at age 3–4.
- Doing arithmetic computations at age 3–4.
- Constantly asking questions at a relatively sophisticated level of understanding.
- Making original (to him) connections between ideas, places, people, and events.
- Displaying an extraordinary memory.
- Exhibiting an unusual ability at drawing, painting, or music.

KINDS OF GIFTEDNESS

Being gifted and talented is not necessarily an across-the-board affair. People can be blessed in various ways. Some children have an extraordinary capacity for mathematics, others for language, others for music. Even "intelligence" is not a single trait—there are many kinds of intelligences, many specific intellectual aptitudes.

In a 1972 report to Congress, then U.S. Commissioner of Education Sidney Marland identified gifted or talented children as those who were exceptionally able in one or more of the following areas:

General intellectual ability
Specific academic aptitude
Creative or productive thinking
Leadership ability
Visual or performing arts
Psychomotor ability

As a parent, you should be alert to whatever gifts or talents your child may possess and work cooperatively with the school to support and nurture them. Watch your child's behavior, especially in his fourth and fifth years. If you suspect unusual talent but are not sure, arrange for individual testing by a competent professional. This person may be a private psychologist or teacher with special training, or, once your child has entered school, the school psychologist. Talk to your child's teacher—she is in a position to observe your child's school behavior every day and to compare it with the behavior of many other children of that age. You have the right to ask the school to conduct special testing if necessary. Try to determine not only whether your child is gifted, but *how* your child is gifted—exactly what are his unusual aptitudes or talents and how extensive are they?

PROGRAMS FOR GIFTED CHILDREN

Practices for educating gifted children in the primary years vary greatly throughout the country. There is no consensus on what should be done, and there exist wide differences in what is and is not done. Although the federal government makes available to the states some funding for this purpose, there is no federal requirement that schools provide services for the gifted, as there is for the handicapped. Some states require that local school districts provide such services; some do not. Some local districts provide them whether required or not; others do not. Some schools have pull-out programs, in which children who are identified as talented are removed from class for a certain time each day or week in order to receive special instruction. These programs may focus on advanced academic skills, provide intellectual stimulation, promote creativity, or all of the above. If they are conducted well, they can challenge your gifted child's imagination and abilities and help keep him from being bored and losing interest.

Many schools like such programs because they are popular, relatively inexpensive, and easy to staff and conduct. But even the best pull-out programs suffer from two limitations: they engage the child for only a portion of the time in school, and they divide, or fragment, his school experience at a time when his emotional needs may require a more constant environment. Gifted children should be continuously challenged throughout the day, not just two or three times a week in small doses. And children in the primary years who are still making an adjustment from home to school may need the reassuring presence of the same group of peers and one nurturing adult in one setting. There will be ample time for special classes in the upper grades.

An alternative to the pull-out approach is to provide enrichment within the regular classroom. Capable teachers at this level can individualize their programs sufficiently to provide for the needs of all but the most extraordinary children. Enrichment should not mean more of the same—the teacher should provide activities that permit greater depth and allow more freedom for the child to use his mind. For example, she can

- Form reading groups or other activity groups according to the children's abilities.
- Conduct individualized reading programs that allow gifted

children to read material well beyond the level of their classmates.

- Assign individual projects to be completed at home or in school with a depth and scope appropriate to the child's abilities.
- Make liberal use of the library—in the school, in the community, at home.
- Provide math games and puzzles that challenge thought and creativity.
- Furnish computer software that permits open-ended inquiry.
- Organize trips to science and art museums.
- Arrange visits by resource people who are able to stimulate the gifted child's curiosity and imagination.

Obviously, these activities can be offered in ways that will make no difference to your child at all. But when they are offered with intelligence and imagination, the authors believe them preferable at this early age to the pull-out programs now in vogue.

HOW CAN PARENTS HELP?

Parents play a critical role in nurturing their children's special gifts or talents. Almost every adult who has been recognized for a rare accomplishment can point to a parent or other adult who identified or encouraged his talent when he was young. The attitudes you foster in your child may be as important in the full development of his talent as the native ability itself. Here are some things you can do to help:

- Talk to your child. Listen to him. Answer his questions. Be interested, be interesting, be patient.

- Read to your child, even though he reads himself. Talk about what you read together.
- Watch television with your child, and help him raise thoughtful and critical questions about what he sees.
- Provide a wide variety of books, games, and puzzles that challenge the mind and the imagination.
- Involve your child in family discussions. Give him a real role to play in family events—counting the change in the store, reading the map on trips.
- Take your child to libraries, museums, concerts, and theatrical events.

As you do these things, remember that however special your child's specific talents may be, he is still a child. He has the same emotional needs as all children—the security of his parents' love and approval, the acceptance of his friends and agemates, and so on. In fact, these needs may be heightened because of his unusual sensitivity and his feeling of being different. At the same time, he must learn to live in a nongifted world. He must be able to get along with people less capable than he. He should not hide his gifts, but he should not expect preferential treatment in all matters because of his ability in some.

You can help by treating your child normally in most situations, by helping him relate to other children who may not be as gifted, by openly discussing his feelings of difference if he brings them up, and by making sure he understands that your love is unconditional and not dependent on his gifts. To be loved, and then to have a special gift, is a wonderful blessing. To go through life feeling that you are more worthy than the gift can be a curse.

HELPFUL RESOURCES

Organizations

American Association for Gifted Children
15 Gramercy Park
New York, New York 10003

Council for Exceptional Children
1820 Association Drive
Reston, Virginia 22091

National Association for Gifted Children
5100 N. Edgewood Drive
Saint Paul, Minnesota 55112

Books

Ehrlich, Virginia Z. *Gifted Children: A Guide for Parents and Teachers.* Englewood Cliffs, N.J.: Prentice-Hall, 1982.

Moore, Linda Perigo. *Does This Mean My Kid's a Genius?* New York: New American Library, Plume, 1982.

Vail, Priscilla L. *The World of the Gifted Child.* New York: Penguin, 1980.

The Child With Learning Problems

The vast majority of children grow and learn without unusual difficulty. They like their teachers, get along with their friends, and make normal progress in their schooling. Some are bright; some less so. Some are early bloomers; some are slower to develop. Some breeze through the work the school assigns; some have more trouble with it. Children in the primary years exhibit a wide range of abilities and states of development. It is well within the normal range for children to have some academic or social difficulty some of the time.

A minority of children is less fortunate. They have been born with handicapping conditions, or have suffered physical or emotional trauma that resulted in such conditions after birth. The parent should know how and where to go to get help for their children in dealing with their handicaps.

Some handicaps are apparent at birth or become evident in early childhood. Severe physical handicaps, blindness, deafness, and mental retardation are in this category. However, other handicapping conditions that impede learning may not surface until the child is in school. Among these conditions are less serious visual and hearing impairments, speech impairment, emotional disturbance, and a variety of problems known collectively as *learning disabilities*. Your child has certain rights to a free, appropriate education regardless of his handicap. Those rights are spelled out later in this chapter. If you are the parent of a severely handicapped child, your problem is beyond the scope of this book. In this chapter we focus on those handicapping conditions most likely to appear once your child has entered school.

SCHOOL-RELATED PROBLEMS

Each year some kindergarten parents receive a message from the school like this: "Mrs. Brown, I'm a little concerned about Johnny. It's the second month of school now, and he still hasn't adjusted to the class. I can't get him to sit still long enough to get involved in his activities, and he disrupts the other children quite a bit. He's fought with two or three of them, and he doesn't seem to be very happy."

Each year some first-grade parents receive a message like this: "Mr. Jones, I think you ought to know that Susie doesn't seem to be learning her reading skills. She's already in the lowest group. She's a lovely child but I can't seem to get her to learn the skills the other children are learning, or even to pay much attention to her work. She tends to spend a lot of time day-dreaming and playing with her braids."

No one likes to receive such messages or worse. If you're normal, you first experience a sick feeling in the pit of your stomach and then a flush of anger—at the school, at your child, or at yourself. To help your child, however, you have to overcome your anger and distress. You have to take charge of yourself and the situation and determine what's wrong and what you're going to do about it.

Problems occur in many forms. Your child may have more than the usual difficulty adjusting to school discipline and routines. He may engage in aggressive or inappropriate behavior with adults or other children. He may be overly shy and withdrawn. He may have great difficulty in learning to read, or he may be able to read but unable to write. He may develop a strong fear or dislike of going to school and revert to infantile behavior at home, such as tantrums or bed-wetting. Or he may simply not be able to do as well in school as his apparent intelligence would indicate.

In an earlier generation children with such problems might have been thought of as slow learners or as being spoiled or lazy. Even today, we encounter children who learn more slowly than others or are spoiled, if not lazy. But in today's world, knowledgeable educators recognize that such behavior is often the sign of a handicapping condition, a condition to which appropriate attention must be paid.

HANDICAPPING CONDITIONS

Among the handicapping conditions that may impede learning and for which help is available under federal law are:

Hearing impairment or deafness
Speech impairment
Visual impairment or blindness
Emotional disturbance
Autism
Mental retardation
Physical impairment
Chronic or long-term health problems
Learning disabilities

The condition need not be especially severe to be handicapping (or to warrant help). Even a mild speech, hearing, or vision problem can affect a child's ability to learn to read and write. An emotional disturbance need not be incapacitating in order to interfere with normal relationships in a classroom. Today, schools are required to identify such conditions and to help children overcome or cope with them, and to involve you as a parent in the decision-making process.

LEARNING DISABILITIES

Most handicapping conditions are readily apparent and easily understood. Once told that a child has a hearing problem, for example, we understand what is meant, even if we may not know exactly what should be done about it. However, one category of handicaps, that of learning disabilities, is not so well understood. It is the most school-related, newest, and rapid-growing of the commonly recognized handicaps. Experts estimate that 1 to 30 percent of the school population have a learning disability of some kind and degree.

The U.S. Department of Education defines learning disabilities as follows:

Specific learning disability means a disorder in one or more of the basic psychological processes involved in understanding or in using language, spoken or written, which disorder may manifest itself in imperfect ability to think, read, write, spell, or do mathematical calculations. The term includes such conditions as perceptual handicaps, brain injury, minimal brain dysfunction, dyslexia, and developmental aphasia. The term does not include children who have learning problems which are primarily the result of visual, hearing, or motor handicaps, of mental retardation, or emotional disturbance, or environmental, cultural, or economic disadvantage.

The breadth and imprecision of this definition reflects the confusion that still exists about why some children have difficulty in learning or in performing certain tasks. Experts are still examining such possible causes as neurological impairment and biochemical irregularities in the body. But for the parent and the teacher, the causes of the problem (and the "labels" that are used once a cause is identified) are much less important than an understanding of what the child can and cannot do and what can and cannot be done to help.

Children with learning disabilities have difficulty with schoolwork for no readily apparent physical or emotional reason. They may be very bright, but there is a decided gap between their apparent ability and their actual achievement. They may be restless, hyperactive, easily distractible. They may be disorganized and careless about things, space, time, work. They may be clumsy and have poor eye-hand coordination. They may have difficulty understanding spoken language, particularly in following directions or understanding requests or questions. They may have difficulty in learning how to read. They may have difficulty in writing what they know or in processing what they hear or read so that they can write about it. They may be able to solve problems but unable to transfer their knowledge to paper in the form of words. They may seem unable to learn number facts or to spell. They may learn things one day and forget them the next. The variety of ability combined with disability is without boundary. Academically or socially or both, they may seem just a bit off-center.

Until a child is about seven or eight years old, it is sometimes difficult to tell whether he suffers from a learning disability or is merely slow to develop. Many children exhibit some of the problems described above and then outgrow them. However, whenever such problems exist, parents and teachers should be aware of them and do what they can to help the child cope, without creating the feeling that something terrible is wrong.

The traditional method of dealing with learning problems is to provide *remediation* in the needed area. For example, if children have poor fine-motor coordination, they are given extensive practice in cutting, tracing, drawing, and the like. Sometimes this focus on a poorly developed skill yields good results. More commonly, however, it leads to increased frustration on the part of all concerned. If the child can't coordinate hand and eye because his nervous system isn't developed that way, no amount of practice will help. We do not ask children who are blind to practice looking at picture books until they can describe the colors. Rather, we help them to develop their sense of hearing.

A more promising and increasingly prevalent approach is to involve the child in many modes of learning using a wide variety of materials, as well as to help him compensate for his weakness rather than to try to eliminate it. A child who is not learning from the basal reading series may learn better from a phonics-oriented program. A child who finds handwriting terribly difficult can type his stories on a typewriter or computer or dictate them to the teacher. If the teacher finds what the child can do well and builds upon it, the child can learn without the emotional damage that often accompanies school failure.

WHEN SHOULD YOU WORRY?

Being the parent of a child with learning problems is not easy. You want to be on top of the situation, to be sure that your child gets whatever help he needs. But you also don't want to make your child distraught by visiting your anxiety upon him. In general, you want to be vigilant but calm. Follow his progress in school closely, and talk with the teacher often. At the first sign of trouble, don't panic. Try to determine the cause, but be sure to be supportive of your child. Build upon the positive. Remember, your child doesn't *want* to have trouble. If *you* don't support him, who will?

Remember, too, that children do not all develop according to the same timetable. Nor are those who develop more quickly necessarily more able when they are grown. Do not be concerned if your child is not reading or writing in kindergarten. (On the other hand, severe behavioral problems, such as hyperactivity or chronic stomach upsets on school days, should be investigated as soon as they appear, even at this early age.) If your child is not making normal progress by the middle of the first-grade year, take steps to find out why. Talk to the teacher and to your pediatrician. If necessary, arrange for testing by a learning disabilities specialist or a school psychologist. And if your child is still not reading or writing toward the end of the second grade, on no account let the year end without obtaining a full diagnosis and a plan for dealing with the problem.

WHAT SHOULD YOU DO? WHAT ARE YOUR RIGHTS?

Federal law gives your child the right to an appropriate education at public expense. The relevant laws are Section 504 of the Rehabilitation Act of 1973, and Public Law 94-142, the Education of All Handicapped Children Act of 1975.

In general, the law requires that your child, regardless of the nature of his handicap, receive a free, appropriate education in as normal a setting as possible (the "least restrictive environment"). Each child must have an Individualized Education Program (IEP), which spells out your child's needs and the details of the educational program devised to deal with those needs. Among the services provided are modification in the regular classroom (such as a computer keyboard or the help of an aide), placement in a resource-room program or special class, counseling and psychological services, social work services, speech and language therapy, medical diagnostic services, transportation, and parent counseling and training. A full evaluation and a new IEP are mandated every three years, and more frequently if you or the teacher requests it.

The law also requires that you as a parent be fully informed of these proceedings and given the opportunity to participate in the decision-making. Before you permit your child to be enrolled in a special program or approve his IEP, be sure you have answers to questions like these:

- What is your child able to do? What is he not able to do? How will the IEP help him learn to do these things?
- What services will your child receive? How exactly will they help him?
- Who will teach or work with your child, and who will be in charge?
- Where will this work be done? When?
- How will your child's progress be evaluated? How will you be involved?

Take the time to find out what your rights are. Two short but excellent documents are

"94-142 and 504: Numbers That Add Up to Educational Rights for Handicapped Children"
Children's Defense Fund
122 C Street, N.W.
Washington, D.C. 20001

"Special Education Checkup: What Federal Law Requires in Educating Your Child"
The National Committee for Citizens in Education
410 Wilde Lake Village Green
Columbia, Maryland 21044

And if you want to read more about children with learning disabilities, we recommend the following:

Clarke, Louise. *How to Overcome Dyslexia in Your Child.* New York: Penguin, 1974.

Osman, Betty B. *Learning Disabilities—A Family Affair.* New York: Random House, 1979.

Osman, Betty, and Blinder, Henriette. *No One to Play With.* New York: Warner, 1986.

"Taking the First Step," Association for Children With Learning Disabilities, 4156 Library Road, Pittsburgh, Pa. 15234.

Communicating With the School

Good schools are those in which parents and teachers work together to help children learn. When the school reflects the values of the home and the home supports the efforts of the school, children grow in an atmosphere of shared purpose and consistent expectations. There is no room for confusion about what is important. The child's total environment reinforces his efforts to achieve what he, his parents, and his teacher all accept as important goals.

Attaining this unity of purpose requires effective communication between home and school. All schools attempt to communicate with parents to some degree; some schools do so better than others, as we shall see. Parents, too, have an obligation to become informed about their own child's progress and about school programs and policies, and to communicate to the school information about their child that can be helpful to the people who work with him.

PARENTS' RIGHTS AND RESPONSIBILITIES

As a parent of a child in school, you have certain rights and responsibilities. You have the right to

- Know what your child is being taught.
- Know how the teacher conducts the class—how she teaches reading, how she groups children for instruction.
- Know how your child is doing—how he gets along with others, how he is progressing in his learning.
- Be told if your child experiences difficulty or seems unhappy.
- Be informed of school policies on such matters as attendance, illness, homework, discipline, and visiting the school.
- Praise and criticize the teacher when appropriate, without fear of reprisal.
- Be spoken to courteously and plainly, without defensiveness or jargon.

You have the responsibility to

- Send your child to school rested, clean, fed, and ready to learn.
- Be aware of your child's work, progress, problems.
- Inform the school if your child has an unusual problem at home.
- Read the material the school sends you—keep yourself informed about school matters.
- Volunteer your time, skills, or resources when they are needed and as you can do so.
- Treat school personnel courteously.

Good schools provide opportunities for the exercise of these rights and responsibilities. They conduct orientation programs for new parents. They hold Open Houses or Back-to-School Nights, at which parents can learn about the school program and meet their child's teacher. They schedule parent-teacher conferences at regular intervals. They call the home when the child is having trouble. They schedule early-morning or evening meetings with parents who work during the day. They include noncustodial parents on their mailing lists (unless a court decree forbids it), and they make step-parents feel welcome. They support volunteer activity and encourage parents to express their views about educational policy. In general, they treat parents as partners in the education of their children.

KNOW YOUR CHILD'S TEACHER

In most states, your child will be with his teacher for the better part of his waking hours for over 180 days each year. That is a long time in his young life, and if things don't go well, it may be a long time in yours.

For these reasons, you should get to know the person who has such influence in your child's life. Plan to meet the teacher at the beginning of the year and on the other occasions that the school provides. Let the teacher know how interested you are in your child's progress. If you have time, drop by the school occasionally—pick your child up at lunch or at the end of the day— and exchange a friendly word or two with the teacher. If you cannot visit the school, write a note to express your appreciation when something nice happens. Call if you have a concern. If you have a problem, don't attack the teacher; describe the situation calmly and ask what the two of you can do together to improve things.

Remember, teachers are people, too, and they are often overworked and harried. Treat them as you would like to be treated, and they will care about your child all the more.

KNOW YOUR CHILD'S PRINCIPAL

Most experts agree that a principal sets the tone of the school. The principal's values, personality, and style of leadership all affect the climate of the building in which your child will spend so much of his young life.

Most children in the primary years will spend little time with the principal. They will probably know the principal's name and what she or he looks like, but little more. Nor is there any reason for you as a parent to push your way into this busy person's life in the first few days of school. But gradually, as months and years go by, you would do well to make the principal's acquaintance, to let the principal know how interested you are in your child's education, and to volunteer your help. (Parents can help in many ways. If you do not have the time to sort books in the school library, you can write a short note to the superintendent praising something that the principal and the teachers have done for your child.) In the normal course of events, the principal will be guiding your child's progress for several years. You should make yourself a partner in the enterprise.

PARENT-TEACHER CONFERENCES

The best way to communicate with the school about your child is to meet directly with the teacher. Face-to-face, you can raise questions and impart useful information about your child, and the teacher can report directly on your child's progress and tell you what you can do to help. Most schools schedule parent-teacher conferences for this purpose. However, if you feel you have a problem and no conference is planned, you should feel free to call the school and ask for one yourself.

How to Prepare for a Conference

In most cases, your time with the teacher will be limited, so it is well to prepare thoroughly in advance. Here are some ways to prepare:

1. Talk to your child. Tell him that you are going to meet with his teacher. Ask him what you should look for in the classroom. See if there are any questions he wants you to ask.
2. Make a list of the questions you want to ask the teacher. They may be general questions: "Is my child working up to ability?" or "How does my child get along with the other children?" Or they may be more specific: "What math book is my child using?" or "May I see something my child has written?"
3. Decide what you want to tell the teacher about your child. If there are unusual family problems that may be affecting your child's behavior, say so, without going into excessive detail. If your child seems bored or anxious, bring the matter up, without accusing the teacher of being the cause.
4. Be prompt. Schools work on tight schedules, and you don't want to lose any of your time or to trespass on the time of others.

How to Participate in a Conference

Many parents are nervous about conferences with a teacher, especially when their children are very young. Remember, the teacher may be nervous, too. Teachers work with children all day, not with adults, and you may represent a threat. The tone to strike is that of a relaxed, confident partner in the child's education. You should be assured without being aggressive, pleasant without being overly deferential. Here are some things to do that may help:

1. Begin the conference on a positive note. Tell the teacher how much your child liked the puppet show in class, or how pleased you are with your child's reading. If you can't think of anything else, thank the teacher for taking the time to see you.
2. Listen carefully to what the teacher has to say. Take notes if you like—they will help you mull things over later.
3. Don't be bashful about saying what you want to say. A good conference involves two-way communication.
4. If the teacher gives you bad news about your child (for example, he behaves immaturely or he doesn't do his work), don't become angry or apologetic. Listen carefully and try to understand. Ask questions like "Could you give me an example?" or "Does it happen often?" Find out what you can do to help. If you don't agree with the teacher, you can deal with that problem later, when there is more time.
5. End the conference on a positive note. Thank the teacher for her time and emphasize the constructive action you are going to take together.

How to Follow Up a Conference

If the conference has been effective, there may be much to think about and discuss later. Here are some steps you might take:

1. Discuss the conference with your child. Emphasize the good things that were said. Be direct about any problems that came up. Be clear about what constructive steps you and your child will be taking to resolve them.
2. Act quickly on any suggestions the teacher has made. If your child's eyes should be tested, make the appointment right away. If there are books you should get at the library, get them.
3. Make sure that your child knows that you and the teacher are working together in his interest. Your child should be secure in

the knowledge that the important adults in his life see eye-to-eye on matters concerning him.

REPORT CARDS

Report cards are the traditional means by which the school communicates in writing about how your child is doing. Especially in these early years, they should be regarded more as a partial description of how your child is developing than as an evaluation of his abilities or achievement.

Schools vary widely in the kinds of report cards they send home. Some provide letter grades and a few short comments; some provide checklists of behavior; some provide written comments only; some use no report cards at all. Figure 1 on page 264 is a typical report card from one suburban school system.

When you receive your child's report card, you should discuss it with him. Ask him how he feels about it. Praise him for what is good, and encourage him to do better with things that need improvement. Find out what you can do to help. And if you are truly concerned, don't hesitate to call for an appointment with your child's teacher. Most teachers will be eager to cooperate with you on the child's behalf.

PUPIL RECORDS

All schools maintain records of their pupils. Almost always, schools record data concerning attendance, health, teacher and room assignments, name and address of parents, and other basic information. They may also record IQ and other test scores, dis-

HOME REPORT OF .... Grade One & Two

Teacher .... Date..

S — Satisfactory Progress
NI — Needs to Improve
* Not applicable at present

STUDY SKILLS	S	NI	COMMENTS
Listens attentively	✓		
Follows directions	✓		
Works independently	✓		
Uses time wisely	✓		
Completes work in reasonable time	✓		

PERSONAL AND SOCIAL GROWTH

	S	NI
Shows self-confidence	✓	
Respects rights and properties of others	✓	
Accepts constructive criticism	✓	

ACADEMIC AREAS

Reading

	S	NI
Enjoys reading	✓	
Understands what he reads	✓	
Applies word attack skills	✓	
Knows vocabulary at his level	✓	
Reads with expression	✓	

WRITTEN EXPRESSION

	S	NI
Uses acceptable forms in handwriting	✓	
Shows original thinking	*	
Conveys ideas in sentences	*	
Spells correctly	*	

ORAL EXPRESSION

	S	NI
Communicates thoughts clearly	✓	
Holds attention of group	✓	

MATHEMATICS

	S	NI
Understands concepts	✓	
Sees relationships	✓	
Solves problems	✓	
Is learning number facts	✓	

SOCIAL STUDIES

	S	NI
Shares experiences and ideas	✓	
Is developing concepts	✓	

SCIENCE

	S	NI
Is acquiring process skills	*	
Participates actively	*	
Understands concepts	*	

COMMENTS:

Beth has made a beautiful adjustment to all first grade activities. She is sweet, cooperative and responsible.

Beth is well organized and is building good work habits She finishes her work quickly and with ease. She will move on independently to productive work. In many cases, she will get involved with extra readers in her free time. She makes good use of our library. She has a very good reading vocabulary and is applying word attack skills to new words. She enjoys and is proud of her accomplishments.

Beth's number concepts progressed slowly at first. Recently she has made good progress in this area, perhaps because of more self confidence She tends to be timid about new academic situations. As learning grows, so will Beth.

She is well liked and respected by her peers.

She is a pleasure to work with.

To report to Room .... in September.

Figure 1.

ciplinary infractions, comments by teachers, or results of psychological testing or appraisal. Figure 2 on page 266 is a fairly typical pupil record form for a child in the primary years.

As a parent you have the right to see any and all records maintained on your child. The federal Family Educational Rights and Privacy Act of 1974, commonly called the Buckley Amendment, provides that parents have

... the right to inspect and review any and all official records, files and data directly related to their children, including all material that is incorporated into each student's cumulative record folder and intended for school use or to be available to parties outside the school or school system, and specifically including but not necessarily limited to identifying data, academic work completed, level of achievement (grades, standardized achievement scores), attendance data, scores of standardized intelligence, aptitude and psychological tests, interest inventory results, health data, family background information, teacher or counselor ratings and observations and verified reports of serious recurrent behavior patterns.

HOMEWORK

As in other matters, schools vary widely in the kind and amount of homework they assign in the primary years. Some give no homework at all. Some give it occasionally, for a particular purpose or occasion. Some give it every day, for up to fifteen or twenty minutes per night.

Good teachers assign homework for a variety of purposes—to have children prepare for an experience ("Bring an apple to school tomorrow"), to practice a skill that has been taught in class

Name: _____ Last _____ First _____ Middle _____ M F _____ School: _____

PUBLIC SCHOOLS

Address _____ City _____ State _____ Zip _____ Telephone _____

Date of Birth _____ Evidence _____ Date of Entrance _____ From _____ Pre-School _____

Parents' Names: Mother _____ Occupation _____ Bus. Phone _____ Father _____ Occupation _____ Bus. Phone _____

With whom does student live at above address _____ Mother _____ Father _____ Other _____ Other tel. and address _____
(Check appropriate people) Specify (if applicable)

Names—Ages of Siblings _____

Transferred To _____ Date _____ Re—Entered From _____ Date _____

Grade	Year	Teacher	Absent	Present	Referral Information

Figure 2.

("Connect the right pictures with the right letters on this sheet"), or to encourge individual creativity or research ("Find a story or a poem about Indians and be ready to tell us about it"). They encourage children to do some work at home, but they don't overburden them. If you feel that your child has too much or too little homework, you may wish to talk to the teacher about it. But unless you are very sure of your ground, it is probably best at this level to let the teacher do things her way.

If your child does receive homework assignments, here are some ways that you can help:

- Provide a quiet, well-lit place. It doesn't need to be a corner of the bedroom or an oak-paneled study—the kitchen table will do just fine. But turn the television off and try to stay off the telephone.
- Establish a regular time. Your child will probably want to unwind when he first comes home from school, but the period just before or just after dinner usually serves well. Make working at this time a habit, and do not deviate unless absolutely necessary.
- Don't let your child dawdle. A thousand excuses to delay work can occur to all of us, and your child is no exception: "I have to sharpen the pencil"; "I need a drink of water"; "The dog wants to go out." One of our favorite teachers began his lecture on study skills with this maxim: "Begin at once." Heed his advice.
- Give your child a notebook or pad for writing down homework assignments. Ask him what the assignment is for the night and help with any unclear directions.
- Ask your child if he needs help. If he does, figure out what to do together with him. If he doesn't, stand back and give him room.
- If your child doesn't mind, check his work and offer questions and suggestions. Help your child to grasp the concept involved as well as to get the right answer. But don't do his work—it is his, not yours.

- Be available to answer questions, but don't hover. Remember, your child is learning to be independent at the same time he is learning math.
- Talk about your child's homework project with the entire family, and get people to contribute ideas.
- Don't become impatient or irritated. If there is a real problem, talk to the teacher. But if for whatever reason your child can't or won't do the work, remember that he is as unhappy about it as you are.

ILLNESS

Most children should go to school most days. However, all of us are prey to occasional colds or stomach upsets, not to mention more serious illness or injury. Here are some things to think about when your child is too ill to go to school:

- Care for your child appropriately, but don't let the day become a treat. You don't want to encourage frequent absence.
- Cooperate with the school's routines. If you are supposed to send in a note the next day, do so. Don't let your busyness or inattention cause your child embarrassment.
- Find your child some lovely books to look at and to read. He may be too sick to go to school, but his mind and his imagination are still active. Don't consign him to a full day of game shows and soap operas.
- If your child is out for more than a day or two, call the teacher and find out what your child is missing. A few days is a long time for a child, and you can help to make it easier when he returns.

If your child complains frequently of illness on school days—stomachaches, headaches, or dizziness are common—talk to him and try to get a sense of what is troubling him. Sometimes children have fears they can't communicate directly to their parents. Perhaps there is a bully on the bus, or a best friend has proved unfaithful. Perhaps he thinks the teacher doesn't like him, or that he can't do the work satisfactorily. Think about any tension in the home that may be affecting your child. If and when you figure things out, be understanding and supportive. Tell your child what you are going to do to help straighten things out. And if you can't determine the cause of the problem, see your teacher and, if necessary, your doctor.

How to Judge a Good Teacher

In schools as we know them, the quality of your child's education depends directly upon the quality of his teacher. No other variable, except possibly the nature of the children in the class, is as important.

As a parent, you have many opportunities to judge the quality of your child's teacher. You talk to your child about his experience in school, you see the work he brings home, you visit the classroom and talk with the teacher. You look for the signs of good teaching described in the earlier chapters of this book. In all these ways you begin to form an impression of this important person in your child's life—a person whose personal characteristics and teaching style shape the environment in which your child lives for a large part of each working day.

WHAT TEACHING IS LIKE

Before thinking about what makes a good teacher, it may be well to consider what the conditions of teaching are like for most classroom teachers.

To begin with, teaching is hard work. It is true that there are long summer vacations and breaks throughout the year. But dealing with a roomful of active children each day is emotionally demanding, exhausting work, involving not only keeping order, but motivating children, planning and conducting dozens of activities, keeping track of individual progress and problems, creating a good feeling in the class as a whole. Most teachers are tired at the end of each day, and for good reason. Think about how you would feel if you had to run a birthday party all day, every day, for several dozen of your child's friends!

Another condition of teachers' lives is that they are constantly with groups of children. They must constantly expend the energy required to maintain discipline in the class. There is little time to be alone, to catch one's breath, and there is little opportunity to interact with other adults. For these reasons, many teachers speak of theirs as a lonely profession—lonely in a crowd.

In many communities, teachers no longer enjoy the respect their predecessors did a generation or more ago. Years ago, the teacher was often one of the most educated and respected people in the community, the person who could read and write and give children the skills to enjoy a future brighter than their parents'. Today, many parents are better educated than their children's teachers, and respect is no longer automatic. (In some states teachers must now take tests to demonstrate their knowledge of their field—and not all teachers pass the tests.) Furthermore, the teacher may be subject to conflicting expectations from different groups of parents. Some may want the teacher to take a more structured, disciplined approach; others may be concerned that the teacher is stifling their children's imagination and creativity.

When you're speaking to your child's teacher, you should keep these and similar considerations in mind. Your empathy will help you establish a relationship that permits effective communication.

WHAT MAKES A GOOD TEACHER

No one style of teaching is best for all children. Just as children vary in their temperament, maturity, abilities, and interests, the kind of teacher who suits the child best also varies. Some children learn more from a teacher who is dynamic, exciting, full of energy. Some respond better to a teacher who is calm, steady, patient. Some profit from a stern taskmaster; others from a kindly, nurturing type. Some do better work with an older teacher; some with a younger. Some work better with a female teacher; some with a male.

To say that good teachers come in many forms is not to say, however, that all teachers are equally good. The teaching profession, like the rest of humankind, has its share of the bright and the dull, the inspired and the flat, the hard-working and the lazy. Most children and parents agree that a good teacher consistently displays the following qualities:

- *Respect* for children. The teacher likes most children, and treats all well.
- *Enthusiasm* for her work. The teacher enjoys what she is doing.
- *Responsibility,* to the children and to the job. Activities are thoughtfully planned; homework is corrected and returned on time.
- *Caring* for individual children. The teacher knows who is struggling and whose spirits are down, and she takes steps to improve things.
- *Fairness* in dealing with the class and with individuals.
- *Friendliness* and overall cheerfulness.
- *Sense of humor* to make things sparkle and to help when things aren't going well.
- *Patience* in dealing with children's difficulties.
- *Skill in communicating,* in understanding what children are thinking and in explaining things well.

- *Knowledge* of the teacher's subject and competence at what she does in the classroom.

Perfect 10's are rare, in teaching as in life. But if your child's teacher comes close, rejoice!

WHAT TO DO ABOUT A BAD TEACHER

Before your child finishes school, he will have many teachers. A few may stand out, the rare people who truly make a positive impression on your child. Most will be just fine, people from whom your child will learn the necessary skills and knowledge and perhaps a thing or two about human nature. And a few may be trouble, people who seem unable to provide a good program for your child or who may cause your child distress. What should you do if you think your child has such a teacher?

What you should *not* do is ignore the situation. Some parents are reluctant to speak to the teacher or the principal because they are afraid the teacher will take out her resentment on the child. In the authors' experience, this fear is prevalent but not well founded. Most teachers do their best to treat their pupils well. And even when a teacher feels resentment, she is apt to change her inappropriate behavior once criticized. Since you should be more interested in appropriate behavior than in good feeling, the criticism is worth making.

The first thing to do is to talk to the teacher. Explain what you think the problem is, and listen to what the teacher has to say. It is true that the teacher may be defensive or resentful, but it is also possible that you may not have all the relevant information. (Remember, your chief source of information is your child, and his version of events, while honest, may not be entirely objective.)

Once you have sorted out in your mind whether there is a

serious problem or not, decide with the teacher what will be done to correct it. Perhaps your child needs to make an adjustment in his behavior. Or perhaps the teacher needs to make an adjustment in hers.

Once you have decided on a course of action, give things time to change. Teachers often respond to such encounters, once they know that a parent is concerned and monitoring the situation. However, if the situation does not improve within a reasonable period of time, your next recourse is to the principal.

You may approach the principal alone or with a small number of other parents who share your concern. (Avoid bringing a large group or "lynch mob"—you may provoke the system to defend itself and frustrate your purpose.) Be specific about your complaints; avoid hearsay and stick to what you know to be true from your own child's experience. Most principals will want to help you solve the problem, particularly if you have talked to the teacher first.

The principal can't do some things, but she can do others. In most states, she can't fire a teacher, at least once the teacher has tenure. (In such states, teachers receive tenure after a probationary period of about three to five years. After that, they may be discharged only for cause, and the legal proceedings are long, difficult, and expensive. Very few tenured teachers are discharged each year, and their cases tend to be extreme.) Nor can the principal, if your school has two classes on a given grade level, assign forty children to one class and ten to the other.

What she can do is meet with the teacher to confront her with the problem and plan a way to resolve it. If the class is too large or too difficult, she may be able to assign a teacher's aide. If supplies are inadequate, she may be able to order more. She can visit the class more often, or get another teacher to do so. She can require the teacher to submit lesson plans, to ensure that adequate planning is being done. If personal problems are interfering with the teacher's effectiveness, she can suggest (or require) counseling help. If the teacher is eligible to retire, the principal can suggest early retirement.

Much of what the principal does, once you leave her office, will not be visible to you. You should not therefore assume that "nothing is being done." Much supervisory work should not be done in public, and most of it takes time. However, if the problem persists beyond a reasonable period, you should not hesitate to call or see the principal again. And if that fails, you should be in touch with the superintendent of schools.

The superintendent is responsible for the operation of the school system as a whole, including the work principals do. Although he will probably not intervene directly in your child's situation, he will do his best to see that the principal and the teacher are doing their jobs properly.

How to Judge a Good School

Schools vary in methods, values, atmosphere, the mix of pupils, resources, size, age, and countless other ways. The authors have seen good schools in factory towns and inner cities and poor schools in affluent suburbs. (We have also seen poor schools in factory towns and inner cities and good schools in affluent suburbs.) How can conscientious parents choose a school that is right for their child? And if choice is not possible, how do parents know whether the school their child attends is good or not?

In the 1960s and 1970s it was fashionable to maintain that schools made little difference in children's lives. Family and economic background were viewed as such powerful forces that schools could do little to help children rise above the circumstances of their home and neighborhood. Today, however, there is increasing evidence that good schools can make a difference. In such schools, children learn to read, write, compute, and think effectively no matter what the social, economic, racial, or ethnic background they and their classmates may have.

EFFECTIVE SCHOOLS RESEARCH

In recent years, researchers have compared schools in which children attain a high level of achievement with lower-achieving schools with children of similar background, identifying the factors that make the good schools so effective. Many individuals and organizations have published lists of such factors. Among the most commonly mentioned are these:

- Effective instructional leadership, usually from a strong principal. The principal sets the tone for the school. If she understands teaching and learning and knows what her goals are, she can influence a school to follow.
- Consensus on goals between the principal, teachers, parents, and pupils. The energies of the entire school should be focused on the same objectives.
- High expectations of achievement. Children tend to work up to what is expected of them. Teachers who expect little, get little; teachers who expect much, given skill on their part and effort all around, get much. Good schools expect children to do well, and they maintain a consistently positive attitude.
- A schoolwide, consistent emphasis on instruction, especially in the basic skills. Teachers work hard at getting children to learn, motivating them, trying different materials and techniques, finding a way for each child to succeed no matter what his difficulties. Teaching and learning are the school's chief priorities.
- Regular assessment of progress. Children are tested often to measure their achievement, and the results are used to guide the instructional plan. The principal and the teacher evaluate their own plan and their own efforts in light of children's achievement.
- A safe, orderly, purposeful climate. The children and adults show respect for one another, and are safe from external disruption.

OTHER INDICATORS OF QUALITY

These factors apply to good schools in all situations. They are receiving increasing attention as the effective schools movement gains momentum. However, there are other traditional indicators of school quality that may make a difference.

Class Size

The research on class size is inconclusive. Studies tend to show that within the limits of about fifteen to thirty children, class size makes little difference in children's achievement. On the other hand, the overwhelming testimony of teachers and parents is that, up to a point, the smaller the class the better. Clearly, the teacher can devote more time to each child if the class is smaller, and there may be advantages for children that are not reflected in the tests. In the primary years, the best class size is probably from fifteen to twenty children. Up to twenty-five, you shouldn't worry; beyond that, you may want to lobby your school to reduce the numbers or to assign additional help, such as a teacher's aide.

Teacher/Pupil Ratio

The teacher/pupil ratio describes the number of pupils in the school or school system for each teacher and other professional staff member. (In a school with 300 children, 15 regular teachers, 3 special teachers, a principal, and a librarian the ratio would be 1/15.) In good schools, there is one professional staff member for every fifteen to twenty children. The number of adults can be increased by assigning teacher aides or parent volunteers.

Special Teachers

Closely related to the pupil/teacher ratio is the number and kinds of special teachers in the school. Some schools have librarians, music teachers, art teachers, physical education teachers, remedial reading teachers, psychologists, and other special services personnel (see the chapter "School Resource People"). Whether or not such services are important depends upon the nature of the children who attend the school and the needs of your own child.

Special Programs

Some schools provide special programs for both handicapped and gifted children (see the chapters "The Gifted Child" and "The Child With Learning Problems"). Some have artists-in-residence, provide special music programs, or offer experimental instruction by computer. Some provide bilingual or English-as-a-second-language instruction. The presence or absence of such programs can make a difference to your child's needs or talents. Look for them when choosing a school; or if your child is already in a school, find out what it offers compared with other schools in the surrounding area.

After-School Activities

Most children in the primary years are ready to go home at the close of the school day. However, in situations where no adult can be at home in the daytime or where children live in relative isolation from potential playmates, some schools offer after-school activity or child-care programs. (Sometimes these programs are conducted by school employees; sometimes they are run by the PTA or a parent cooperative.) Discover what your school offers to help meet your family's needs.

Budget

School budgets vary widely from one area of the country to another, depending upon the regional cost of living and the way school expenses are financed. Here are a few rules of thumb you can apply to determine whether your school is funded adequately:

- What is your school's expenditure per pupil? If it is below average for your region, why? What is your child not receiving that other children are?
- What is your teacher/pupil ratio? Again, if it is below average for your region, why? What services do other children receive that your child does not?
- Do teachers come to your school district from other districts, or do they leave to go elsewhere? How do salaries and fringe benefits compare?
- Do teachers have all the books and supplies they need, or must they cut back on what the children do?

WHAT TO LOOK FOR WHEN YOU VISIT A SCHOOL

The preceding comments should suggest some of the questions to ask at PTA or Board of Education meetings, or to research with appropriate school officials. However, you can learn a lot just by taking the time to visit the school and look around. Here are a dozen questions that may help you:

- Is the building open to you? Do you get the sense that visitors are frequent and welcome? Or do locked doors and forbidding signs suggest otherwise?
- How do the secretaries treat you? Are you made to feel com-

fortable and welcome? Or are you eyed with indifference or suspicion?

- How do the children behave? Do they seem to know what they are doing, and are they going about it freely and easily? Is the atmosphere too loose or too rigid?
- How do the teachers behave? Do they seem to enjoy what they are doing? At lunch or recess, do they interact with the children or do they stand apart and talk to one another?
- Is the building clean, well-lit, and in good repair?
- Are there separate facilities for music, art, and physical education? Are they in use?
- Is children's work—artwork, poetry, and other writing—displayed in the halls and classrooms? Does it look recent? Does it look as if someone cared?
- Are the children's bathrooms clean and accessible? Are they properly supplied?
- Is there a school library (and a librarian)? Is it well stocked? Are books attractively displayed? Are there children in the library? Are they working both alone or in small groups and as a class? (If there are no children in the library when you visit, ask how and when children come there.)
- Are the classrooms busy and inviting, with materials and displays suggesting that much is going on? Is there a hum of activity?
- Do the classrooms contain textbooks and other instructional materials on many levels, to accommodate children's different levels of ability and interests?
- Are most books copyrighted within the past five years?

Every school building has a distinctive ethos, or climate, the product of the kind of people who work there, the nature of the community, and the quality of the leadership. By spending some time in the school and checking against the above list, you will come away with a fairly good feel for the school. If you are choosing a school, trust your instincts. Remember, in the final analysis, a good school is one that is good for your child.

School Resource People

In the chapter "How to Judge a Good Teacher," we discussed classroom teachers, the most important people in your child's school life. In the chapter "How to Judge a Good School," we covered class size, pupil/teacher ratios, and school budgets. In this chapter, we will write about the other school employees whose presence or absence, kindness or indifference, skill or lack of it, may make an important difference to your child.

Not all schools have all the personnel described below. Elementary schools vary widely in size and financial resources, and children in different neighborhoods vary in their needs. Many schools have only classroom teachers, a principal, a secretary, a nurse, one or more custodians, and perhaps a librarian. But where there are other personnel, you should know who they are, what they do, and how you can call upon them in your child's interests.

THE PRINCIPAL

The principal is the key authority figure in the school. She decides on teacher and pupil assignments, evaluates the teachers, allocates the funds provided by the superintendent and the Board

282

of Education, develops the schedules and routines by which the school operates, and administers discipline when necessary. She also, if she is good, leads her staff and parent body in formulating and carrying out an instructional plan for the entire school. Many experts agree that the principal sets the tone for the entire school. Without a good principal, schools are rarely successful.

ASSISTANT PRINCIPALS

In very large elementary schools there may be one or more assistant principals who help the principal in carrying out her duties. The role of the assistant principal is often specialized, depending upon her individual talents and the needs of the situation. For example, an assistant principal might be in charge of discipline, transportation, and the lunch program. Or she might spend the bulk of her time observing and evaluating teachers, and working with committees to improve the instructional program.

THE NURSE

Other than the classroom teacher, the school nurse is the person you may come to know best, particularly if your child has a physical or emotional problem. She may also be the person your child meets first, because one of her duties is to check the health of all children new to the school. After that, she maintains each child's health record, including immunizations and the results of vision, hearing, and medical examinations. She advises teachers on any necessary adjustments to make because of a child's health status. She brings safety conditions to the attention of the principal. She may teach a portion of the school's health program.

And most important, it is to her that your child will go when he is sick, injured, or upset. A good nurse must not only have good first-aid skills, she must be part psychologist, part detective, part mother. In cases when there are no adults at home in the daytime, it is especially important that a sick, injured, or upset child have a skilled and caring nurse to turn to.

THE SCHOOL PHYSICIAN

Most school physicians, where they exist, are employed on a part-time basis. As a result, the functions they perform are limited. They may perform medical examinations when the child has not been examined privately. They provide information to the nurse as needed. They furnish advice about the school's health program. They assist teachers and others in reviewing the placement and program of children who may have handicapping conditions.

If your child is referred to the school physician, make it your business to find out why without delay.

THE SCHOOL SECRETARY

The school secretary does a great deal more than type the principal's letters and get the coffee. She answers the telephone, furnishes information and advice, greets visitors, finds lost lunches and rain boots, delivers a thousand messages each day, settles disputes between teachers, and generally keeps things glued together and operating. Next to the principal, the school secretary is most responsible for the tone of the school.

THE CUSTODIAN

The custodian, too, does more than sweep the floors and take out the trash. First, he knows a lot about what goes on in the school—unlike the teachers and perhaps the principal, he is in most classrooms each day, and he is in a position to know the seamy underside of school life. Second, he is often an important male figure for boys otherwise surrounded by girls and women. And finally, if he likes children, as many do, and is of an amiable disposition, he can be a valuable help in carrying out school projects and activities.

THE LIBRARIAN

The school that has a good librarian is truly blessed. She is much more than the keeper of the books. Her greatest pleasure is in getting children to enjoy reading. She knows the books in her collection, and is always ready to tell you about her favorites. She knows the children in the school—by name, by interest, by level of reading ability—and she helps them find books that stir their imagination and whet their appetite for more. She reads to the children. She consults with the teacher and brings books to class. She makes the school library a warm, inviting place. She is a joy in your child's life. Get to know her, and if you have time, help her out.

ART, MUSIC, AND PHYSICAL EDUCATION TEACHERS

Some schools have teachers with special training in art, music, or physical education. They teach the class once or more per week while the regular classroom teacher helps out, prepares lessons, or takes a break. If the school is small, they may be shared with one or more other schools. These teachers can add expert knowledge to the program, but they are not likely to be important figures to your child at this age.

READING AND SPECIAL EDUCATION TEACHERS

Reading teachers are specially trained to help children with learning problems to improve their reading skills. They typically work with an individual child or a small group of children, diagnosing individual problems and providing remedial help. The children leave the regular classroom and go to the reading teacher for that purpose. The reading teacher also works with regular classroom teachers, helping them to plan and conduct their reading programs.

Special education teachers, like reading teachers, are specially trained to diagnose and deal with individual learning problems. However, their scope is somewhat broader, including writing, math, study skills, and other parts of the curriculum. They may work with a small class for the entire day (in a self-contained class), or they may deal with individual or small groups of children who come to their room at certain times (in a resource room program). They are especially helpful with children who have learning disabilities (see the chapter "The Child With Learning Problems.")

SPEECH TEACHER

Sometimes called a speech therapist or a speech clinician, the speech teacher works with individuals or small groups of children on a wide range of speech and language problems, including stuttering, lisping, poor articulation, or other language disorders. She also advises regular teachers on techniques to use with children in their classrooms who have speech or language problems. If your child is referred to a speech teacher, you should communicate with school authorities to find out about the exact nature of the problem.

THE SCHOOL PSYCHOLOGIST

The school psychologist administers tests to determine children's needs, abilities, and progress. She interprets test results for teachers and parents, and recommends appropriate instructional settings and techniques. She helps individual children with school adjustment problems. If children are not doing well academically, she tries to determine why. She is not a psychiatrist, and she does not provide therapy. If your child is referred to a psychologist, approach her as a possible source of help, but make it your business to find out the reason for the referral. And remember that you have the right to be treated as a full partner in your own child's education.

THE SCHOOL SOCIAL WORKER

The school social worker provides a special link between school and home. She helps children and their families deal with problems that affect learning, such as problems of attendance, school adjustment, peer relationships. She suggests helpful resources. She provides short-term counseling on school-related problems. She acts as an advocate for the child, helping the family understand the school and the school to understand the family.

TEACHER'S AIDES

Teacher's aides may be hired to assist teachers in classrooms, to supervise lunch or recess, to work in the school library, or to help out in many other ways. They are usually people who like children and who have much to offer but who do not have the required license to teach. They can be very important to your child. Get to know the aides who deal with your child directly.

COORDINATORS

Some school districts have coordinators of subjects, such as art, music, science, and reading. Normally these people are assigned to the central administrative offices and visit local schools periodically. They are responsible for planning the curriculum, supervising teachers, and providing instructional support in their subject areas. Your child is not likely to know them, but you may wish to know who they are in the event that you have a question about curriculum that your principal cannot answer.

THE SUPERINTENDENT OF SCHOOLS

The superintendent of schools is the chief executive officer of the school district. On all matters pertaining to the routine operation of the schools, the buck stops with him. Chances are, however, that you will never have occasion to deal with him or her, unless you become involved in a controversy of district-wide proportions, such as a school closing. The superintendent is nonetheless an important figure behind the scenes of your child's life, because he or she controls resources, appoints staff members, and sets a tone that affects the climate of the schools under his or her control.

THE BOARD OF EDUCATION

Most school districts are governed by lay Boards of Education elected by the people. Boards have the final authority in school matters. They appoint the superintendent, establish policy, and oversee the overall long-term operation of the school district. They exert an important influence on the character and quality of the school district.

How to Improve Your School

The authors have spent their lives working with the teachers and other people who work in schools. By and large, we like school people. As a group, they are honest and more likely to be concerned about the welfare of others than the average person in many lines of work. And in general, they do a good job. For all its shortcomings, our system of public schools has indeed educated the masses and helped us create one people out of many.

At the same time, we have never seen a school that couldn't be improved. And the key to improvement is usually the involvement of an active, knowledgeable parent body. A wise school superintendent once said that "schools rarely rise above the expectations of the people who support them." If you want your child's school to be good, you and your friends and neighbors had better get involved.

As an individual, you can read the school's material, get to know the school staff, join the PTA and work on its committees, volunteer to help in classrooms or the library, attend Board of Education meetings, ask questions, and make your opinions known. Some schools involve parents on curriculum committees (parents help decide *what* should be taught, teachers decide *how*) and on screening committees to interview new teachers or aides. Some schools have parent advisory committees that meet regularly with the principal to review all aspects of the school program

290

or to monitor the progress of a new program (such as an extended-day kindergarten program or a new bilingual approach to instruction). Join such groups. The more informed and active you become, the more your influence will grow.

However, you can accomplish much more by working cooperatively with others. If you have a problem that is not limited only to your child, express your views to other parents and see if they feel the same. Then join together as a group—within the PTA, if the leaders will support you; as a separate group, if for some reason the PTA leaders won't go along—and approach the school authorities to seek relief.

Perhaps the school has a teacher who is consistently not effective or who is mean to children. Perhaps the principal is weak or tired or doesn't like the children who have moved to the neighborhood. Perhaps the playground needs repair. Perhaps the school's reading scores are low, or the programs in art or music are unimaginative, or the library is too much off limits, or there are no provisions made for gifted children. Whatever the problem, organize yourself and others to address it. The following steps may help:

1. Get your facts straight. Don't rely on hearsay; speak from first-hand experience. If your problem involves statistical information, such as test scores or budget accounts, do your homework. Nothing will weaken your argument more than seeming not to know what you're talking about.
2. Define your solutions. It is not enough to complain; you must say what you want. If the class size is too large, do you want a teacher's aide or do you want to split the class and hire another teacher?
3. Get your group together. Make sure that everyone understands what the issues are and what solutions you are proposing. Never argue among yourselves before the school authorities.
4. Approach the appropriate level of authority. If the problem is one the teacher can correct herself (even if you think she won't), see the teacher first. If the teacher doesn't resolve the

problem or if the problem is beyond the scope of her authority, see the principal. And if the problem is district-wide in scope or if it requires resources that the principal does not command, see the superintendent or the Board of Education.

5. Be polite but firm. You may wish to write a letter first or to talk on the telephone, but the best way to resolve a problem is to talk face-to-face. Let the school authorities know that you are counting on them to resolve the problem but that you mean business and are not going to go away.

6. Persist. Don't be put off by jargon or evasiveness or the attitude that the issue is none of your business. It *is* your business if it involves your child. And don't be derailed by unnecessary delays. In fairness, some problems cannot be solved immediately, and not all that the school authorities do will be visible to you. But if you do not get satisfaction in a reasonable period of time, return to ask why.

7. If necessary, raise the ante. Most school problems can be resolved cooperatively if parents and school people show a little skill and patience and a willingness to try. But in particularly difficult situations, confrontation may be necessary. Get some teachers on your side. Write to the local newspaper. Organize a crowd at the next meeting of the Board of Education. Talk about a boycott.

In the authors' experience, most situations need never get that far. Reasonable people on both sides can achieve much without letting things get out of hand. If the school authorities are willing to be accommodating, don't push too hard, even if you don't get everything you want. The object is to improve the school, not to win a battle.

The National PTA publishes the handbook *Looking in on Your School, a Workbook for Improving Public Education.* Write to:

The National PTA
700 North Rush Street
Chicago, Illinois 60611-2571

The National Committee for Citizens in Education (NCCE) publishes several useful pamphlets, including "Effective Schools: How to Evaluate Them, How to Get Them," "Finding Out How People Feel About Local Schools," "Parents Organizing to Improve Schools," and "Your School: How Well Is It Working?" Include $1.00 handling charge for each order, and write to:

NCCE
410 Wilde Lake Village Green
Columbia, Maryland 21044

Some of the Authors' Favorite Books for Reading Aloud

Reading aloud to your child is a pleasure to maintain as long as possible. Long after your child is a proficient reader, you should still read aloud to him. Reading aloud is a wonderful way to be close to your child, as well as a way to enjoy literature and art. Some of the most beautiful art today can be found in children's picture books. Give yourself an excuse to sit down with your child and enjoy a good story and lovely illustrations. Just because your child grows older and more mature, don't give up reading picture books. Part of the pleasure in writing this book was the opportunity to review old favorite books and discover magnificent new ones.

The following is a list, limited by necessity, of some of the authors' favorite books for reading aloud. Some of the books you can read at one sitting. The longer books may take weeks or even longer, if you read a chapter at a time. Many of the authors on the list have written other books that are also treasures. We have included the phrase *and more* if the title character appears in other books by the author. When they are available, we have listed the paperback editions.

SHORT BOOKS

Aardema, Verna. *What's So Funny, Ketu?* Illustrated by Marc Brown. New York: Dial Press, 1982.
Ketu has a special gift: the ability to hear animals think.

Aardema, Verna. *Why Mosquitos Buzz in People's Ears.* Illustrated by Leo and Diane Dillon. New York: Dial Press, 1978.
A West African tale about a mosquito who tells a tall tale and makes trouble in the jungle. Stunning full-color pictures.

Aliki. *Wild and Wooly Mammoths.* New York: Harper & Row, Trophy, 1983.
About the life of the wooly mammoth and the people who hunted them thousands of years ago.

Allard, Harry. *Miss Nelson Is Missing* (and more). Illustrated by James Marshall. New York: Scholastic, 1978.
Miss Nelson, the sweet-voiced teacher of the class in Room 207, is replaced by unpleasant Miss Viola Swamp.

Andersen, Hans Christian. *The Ugly Duckling.* Retold and illustrated by Lorinda Bryan Cauley. New York: Harcourt Brace Jovanovich, Voyager, 1979.
The traditional tale of the ugly duckling who turns into a beautiful swan. Told beautifully, with lovely illustrations.

Barrett, Judi. *Cloudy With a Chance of Meatballs.* Illustrated by Ron Barrett. New York: Atheneum, 1978.
The weather changes for the worse in Chewandswallow, a town where it rains soup and juice and the wind blows in frankfurters. Distinctive and original illustrations.

Baylor, Byrd. *Hawk, I'm Your Brother.* Illustrated by Peter Parnall. New York: Scribners, 1976.
Lyric prose about a young native American boy who wants to fly. He steals a baby hawk but finally lets it go so that the hawk can fly for both of them.

Bemelmans, Ludwig. *Madeline* (and more). New York: Penguin, Puffin Books, 1977.
Madeline, a little girl who lives with eleven other little girls in an old house in Paris, has her appendix out.

Blume, Judy. *The Pain and the Great One.* Illustrated by Irene Trivas. Scarsdale, N.Y.: Bradbury Press, 1984.
A six-year-old boy (the pain) and an eight-year-old girl (the great one) comment on each other. Delightful illustrations.

Brown, Margaret Wise. *Goodnight Moon.* Illustrated by Clement Hurd. New York: Harper & Row, Trophy, 1977.
Sheer poetry. A pleasure for any child and every adult.

Brown, Marcia. *Cinderella.* New York: Scribners, 1954.
Magical pastel illustrations go hand in hand with the old story told well.

Burton, Virginia Lee. *Life Story.* Boston: Houghton Mifflin, 1962.
A marvelous account of the changing earth in geologic terms from the beginning of time till today. An unusual book, with marvelous illustrations.

Burton, Virginia Lee. *The Little House.* Boston: Houghton Mifflin, 1978.
Beautifully illustrated story about a little house that is built way out in the country, almost ends up in the city, but makes an unexpected escape back.

Burton, Virginia Lee. *Mike Mulligan and His Steam Shovel.* Boston: Houghton Mifflin, 1977.
To everyone's surprise, Mike Mulligan and his steam shovel, Mary Anne, build the cellar for the new Popperville town hall in one day.

Clark, Mary Lou. *Dinosaurs.* Chicago: Children's Press, 1981.
Dinosaurs, what came before and after them, why they disappeared, and how we know about them.

De Brunhoff, Jean. *The Story of Babar* (and more). New York: Random House, 1937.
After an adventure in the city, Babar and Celeste are crowned King and Queen of the elephants.

De Paola, Tomie. *Strega Nona* (and more). Englewood Cliffs, N.J.: Prentice-Hall, Treehouse, 1975.
An old tale about a magical pasta pot. Charming illustrations.

Flack, Marjorie. *Angus and the Ducks* (and more). Garden City, N.Y.: Doubleday, 1930.
Angus loses his curiosity for a little while after his run-in with some ducks.

Flack, Marjorie. *The Story About Ping.* Illustrated by Kurt Wiese. New York: Penguin, Puffin Books, 1977.
Ping, a young Peking duck, finds himself in serious trouble when he doesn't return to his houseboat on time.

Freeman, Don. *Corduroy.* New York: Penguin, Puffin Books, 1976.
An appealing toy bear who is missing a button finds a home with a little girl.

Freeman, Don. *Dandelion.* New York: Penguin, Puffin Books, 1977.
Dandelion gets his mane curled for Jenniffer Giraffe's tea-and-taffy party.

Freeman, Don. *Norman the Doorman.* New York: Penguin, Puffin Books, 1981.
Norman, a doorman for mice at the basement door of the Majestic Museum of Art, wins a very special contest.

Friedman, Ina. *How My Parents Learned to Eat.* Illustrated by Allen Say. Boston: Houghton Mifflin, 1984.
A little girl's story of how her Japanese mother and American sailor father met and married.

Gág, Wanda. *Millions of Cats.* New York: Coward, McCann & Geohegan, 1977.
A lonely old couple long for a cat and almost end up with trillions of them.

Galdone, Paul. *Three Billy Goats Gruff.* Boston: Houghton Mifflin, 1981.
The illustrations of the troll under the bridge are simply marvelous in this classic tale.

Garrison, Christian. *The Dream Eater.* Illustrated by Diane Goode. Scarsdale, N.Y.: Bradbury Press, 1978.
As beautiful as an Oriental scroll, this book is a wonderful tale of the baku—a dream eater who likes nightmares best.

Goble, Paul. *Buffalo Woman.* Scarsdale, N.Y.: Bradbury Press, 1984.
An old Native American legend that tells the love story between a young brave and a beautiful young woman who is really a female buffalo. Fantastic color illustrations.

Goble, Paul. *The Gift of the Sacred Dog.* Scarsdale, N.Y.: Bradbury Press, 1984.
This is a lovely tale celebrating the native American's love for the horse. Splendid illustrations.

Goble, Paul. *The Girl Who Loved Wild Horses.* Scarsdale, N.Y.: Bradbury Press, 1978.
A native American girl's love for horses leads her to go live with them. Illustrated with beautiful paintings.

Gramatky, Hardie. *Little Toot* (and more). New York: Putnam, 1978.
Little Toot, the little tugboat who would rather play than work, comes of age when he helps to save a giant ocean liner.

Grimm. *The Fisherman and His Wife.* Translated by Randall Jarrell; illustrated by Margot Zemach. New York: Farrar, Straus and Giroux, 1980.
Beautiful illustrations enhance this wonderful translation of the story about a fisherman who has a wife who is *never* satisfied and always wants more.

Hoban, Russell. *Bread and Jam for Frances* (and more). Illustrated by Lillian Hoban. New York: Harper & Row, 1964.
Frances, the little badger, finally gets tired of bread and jam and tries Mother Badger's spaghetti and meatballs.

Ike, Jane Hori, and **Baruch, Zimmerman.** *A Japanese Fairy Tale.* Illustrated by Jane Hori Ike. New York: Warne, 1982.
Beautiful watercolor illustrations. Lovely tale of the love between a beautiful woman and her ugly husband.

Isadora, Rachel. *Ben's Trumpet.* New York: William Morrow, Greenwillow, 1979.
Wonderful black and white illustrations help to tell the story of a little boy who wants to play the trumpet but only has an imaginary instrument.

Keats, Ezra Jack. *A Snowy Day.* New York: Penguin, Puffin Books, 1976.
A boy, a fresh snow, and spectacular illustrations.

Keats, Ezra Jack. *Peter's Chair.* New York: Harper & Row, Trophy, 1983.
Peter has a new sister. She's in his old cradle—and his parents have painted it pink!

Keats, Ezra Jack. *A Letter to Amy.* New York: Harper & Row, Trophy, 1984.
Peter sends a special letter to Amy and hopes for the best.

Leaf, Munro. *The Story of Ferdinand.* Illustrated by Robert Lawson. New York: Penguin, Puffin Books, 1977.
A peace-loving bull would rather smell the flowers than fight in bullfights.

Marshall, James. *George and Martha* (and more). Boston: Houghton Mifflin, Sandpiper, 1974.
A book of five little tales about two good friends who happen to be hippopotamuses.

McCloskey, Robert. *Lentil.* New York: Penguin, 1978.
Lentil and his harmonica become heros in their hometown of Alto, Ohio.

McCloskey, Robert. *Make Way for Ducklings.* New York: Penguin, Puffin Books, 1976.
Mr. and Mrs. Mallard and their eight ducklings find a new home in the Public Garden in Boston, but then Mrs. Mallard has to lead them through Boston from their nest on the Charles River.

Miles, Miska. *Annie and the Old One.* Illustrated by Peter Parnall. Boston: Little, Brown/Atlantic Monthly Press, 1971.
Poignant tale of relationship between a young native American girl and her grandmother.

Minarik, Else Holmelund. *Little Bear* (and more). Illustrated by Maurice Sendak. New York: Harper & Row, 1978.
Four simple but charming stories about a little bear and his family.

Mosel, Arlene. *Tikki Tikki Tembo.* Illustrated by Blair Lent. New York: Scholastic, 1984.
An old tale that explains why the Chinese give their children little short names rather than great big long ones.

Parish, Peggy. *Amelia Bedelia* (and more). Illustrated by Fritz Siebel. New York: Harper & Row, 1983.
Hilarious misadventures of a lovable maid who is very creative when she follows Mrs. Rogers's housekeeping directions.

Piper, Watty. *The Little Engine That Could.* Illustrated by George and Doris Hauman. New York: Scholastic, 1979.
When the big trains break down, the little blue engine comes through courageously.

Rey, H. A. *Curious George* (and more). Boston: Houghton Mifflin, Sandpiper, 1973.
The rollicking adventures of a curious monkey who goes to live in the zoo after he is captured by the man in the yellow hat.

Sendak, Maurice. *Where the Wild Things Are.* New York: Harper & Row, Trophy, 1984.
Max has a wonderful fantasy about a magical land inhabited by wild and terrible creatures.

Seuss, Dr. *And to Think I Saw It on Mulberry Street.* New York: Vanguard, 1937.
The wonderful things that little Marco "sees" on Mulberry Street. Charming rhymes and pictures.

Silverstein, Shel. *The Giving Tree.* New York: Harper & Row, 1964.
The loving gifts a tree gives to a young boy as he grows from boyhood to maturity and finally into old age.

Simon, Seymour. *The Smallest Dinosaurs.* Illustrated by Anthony Rao. New York: Crown, 1982.
Descriptions and illustrations of seven small dinosaurs believed to be the ancestors of today's birds.

Slobodkin, Esphyr. *Caps for Sale.* New York: Scholastic, Blue Ribbon, 1984.
A tale about a peddler, his caps, and some very mischievous monkeys.

Steig, William. *The Amazing Bone.* New York: Penguin, Puffin Books, 1977.
Suspenseful tale of a magical and powerful bone.

Steig, William. *Sylvester and the Magic Pebble.* New York: Simon and Schuster, Windmill Books, 1969.
Sylvester the donkey finds a wonderful magic pebble that gets him into terrible trouble.

Thompson, Kay. *Eloise.* Illustrated by Hilary Knight. New York: Simon and Schuster, 1969.
The story of Eloise, who lives in the elegant Plaza Hotel in New York.

Udry, Janice M. *Let's Be Enemies.* Illustrated by Maurice Sendak. New York: Harper & Row, 1981.
John goes to James's house to tell him that he's not his friend anymore, but their friendship is so strong that they end up roller-skating together.

Ungerer, Tomi. *Crictor.* New York: Harper & Row, 1983.
About Madame Bodot's pet boa constrictor.

Van Allsburg, Chris. *The Polar Express.* Boston: Houghton Mifflin, 1985.
A little boy takes a fantastic trip to the North Pole and the Polar Express. Mysterious large illustrations.

Yagawa, Sumiko. *The Crane Wife.* Translated by Katherine Paterson. Illustrated by Sue Kichi Akaba. New York: William Morrow, 1981.
One of Japan's most beloved folktales with magnificent traditional illustrations.

Yashima, Taro. *Crow Boy.* New York: Penguin, Puffin Books, 1976.
A tale set in Japan about a shy little boy who outgrew his nickname of Chibi, or Tiny Boy, and became Crow Boy, who is loved and admired by all.

Yashima, Taro. *Umbrella.* New York: Penguin, Puffin Books, 1977.
A beautifully illustrated story about the first day Momo used her umbrella.

Yolen, Jane. *Sleeping Ugly.* Illustrated by Diane Stanley. New York: Putnam, 1981.
A delightful tale of the beautiful but unpleasant Princess Miserella and of Plain Jane, who has a face to match her name but a loving and appealing personality.

Zion, Gene. *Harry the Dirty Dog* (and more). Illustrated by Margaret B. Graham. New York: Harper & Row, Trophy, 1976.
Wonderfully illustrated story of a little white dog with black spots who hates soap and water.

Zolotow, Charlotte. *My Grandson Lew.* Illustrated by William Pène du Bois. New York: Harper & Row, Trophy, 1985.
Lewis and his mother share the wonderful memories they both have of his grandfather and the love he brought to them.

LONGER BOOKS

Atwater, Richard, and Florence Atwater. *Mr. Popper's Penguins.* Illustrated by Robert Lawson. New York: Dell, 1978.
Hilarious story of a house painter who adds twelve penguins to his household.

Baum, L. Frank. *The Wonderful Wizard of Oz.* New York: Penguin, Puffin Books, 1983.
The story of Dorothy and her comrades on their way to the Emerald City is as captivating as ever.

Blume, Judy. *Freckle Juice.* Illustrated by Sonia O. Lisker. New York, Dell, 1978.
A hilarious story about a boy who wants to have freckles.

Bond, Michael. *A Bear Called Paddington* (and more). Illustrated by Peggy Fortnum. Boston: Houghton Mifflin, 1960.
Paddington, a bear from Darkest Peru, comes to live with the Brown family and causes delightful havoc.

Cleary, Beverly. *Henry Huggins* (and more). Illustrated by Louis Darling. New York: Dell, Yearling Books, 1979.
Henry meets a stray dog in the drugstore, names him Ribsy, and brings him home. Together they start their adventures.

Cleary, Beverly. *Ramona the Pest* (and more). Illustrated by Louis Darling. New York: Dell, Yearling Books, 1982.
Spunky Ramona, Henry Huggins's little sister, enters kindergarten.

Dahl, Roald. *Charlie and the Chocolate Factory.* New York: Bantam-Skylark, 1981.
About Charlie and his friends, and Mr. Willy Wonka's Chocolate Factory. Filled with suspense and humor.

Dahl, Roald. *James and the Giant Peach.* Illustrated by Nancy Ekholm Burkert. New York: Bantam-Skylark, 1981.
James, an orphan who is treated cruelly, escapes into a giant peach that is growing in his backyard, where he meets a cast of intriguing characters.

Estes, Eleanor. *The Hundred Dresses.* Illustrated by Louis Slobodkin. New York: Harcourt, Brace & World, 1968.
Wanda lives on the wrong side of town and wears the same faded blue dress to school every day. When her classmates tease her, she tells them that she has a hundred dresses in her closet at home.

Estes, Eleanor. *The Moffats* (and more). Illustrated by Louis Slobodkin. New York: Harcourt, Brace & World, 1968.
The four Moffat children and their mother don't have much money but they do have good times together.

Fitzhugh, Louise. *Harriet the Spy.* New York: Dell, 1984.
An only child and a little bit lonely, Harriet keeps a notebook of what she observes about her parents, classmates, and neighbors.

Grahame, Kenneth. *The Wind in the Willows.* Illustrated by John Burningham. New York: Penguin, Puffin Books, 1984.
Wonderful humor and sensitivity live on in this classic tale of the joy of simple life in the forest.

Greene, Constance. *A Girl Called Al* (and more). Illustrated by Byron Barton. New York: Dell, Yearling Books, 1977.
Al is a little bit fat, is the child of divorced parents, and claims to be a nonconformist. The warm and funny story of a friendship between two girls who live in an apartment house.

Lawson, Robert. *Ben and Me.* New York: Dell, Yearling Books, 1973.
Wonderfully entertaining biography of Benjamin Franklin written by his good friend Amos the mouse, who claims to be largely responsible for Franklin's inventions and discoveries. Appealing drawings.

Lindgren, Astrid. *Pippi Longstocking* (and more). Translated by Florence Lamborn; illustrated by Louis S. Glanzman. New York: Penguin, Puffin Books, 1977.
The fantastic adventures of independent, idiosyncratic redheaded Pippi.

MacLachlan, Patricia. *Sarah, Plain and Tall.* New York: Harper & Row, 1985.
Caleb's mother died a day after he was born and his papa places an ad in the newspaper for a new wife. Sarah answers the ad and comes in the spring with her cat, Seal.

McCloskey, Robert. *Homer Price.* New York: Penguin, Puffin Books, 1976.
Zany episodes in the life of a small-town American boy.

Milne, A. A. *Winnie-the-Pooh* (and more). Illustrated by Ernest H. Shepard. New York: Dell, Yearling Books, 1970.
Classic story of Christopher Robin and his wonderful friends.

Sobol, Donald J. *Encyclopedia Brown, Boy Detective* (and more). New York: Bantam, 1978.
Adventures of a famous boy detective who gives the reader an opportunity to solve mysteries.

Taylor, Sydney. *All-of-a-kind Family* (and more). Illustrated by Beth and Joe Krush. New York: Dell, 1966.
Life with a Jewish family in New York at the turn of the century. Warmly told.

Travers, P. L. *Mary Poppins* (and more). Illustrated by Mary Shepard. New York: Harcourt Brace Jovanovich, 1981.
Delightful nonsense about a remarkable nursemaid who blew in with the east wind.

Warner, Gertrude Chandler. *The Boxcar Children.* Niles, Ill.: Albert Whitman, Pilot, 1977.
Four orphans determined to care for themselves find a home in a boxcar.

White, E. B. *Charlotte's Web.* Illustrated by Garth Williams. New York: Harper & Row, Trophy, 1952.
The powerful relationship between two barnyard animals: Wilbur, a pig, and Charlotte, a spider.

White. E. B. *Stuart Little.* Illustrated by Garth Williams. New York: Harper & Row, Trophy, 1945.
The charming adventures of an engaging mouse. A classic.

White, E. B. *The Trumpet of the Swan.* Illustrated by Edward Frascino. New York: Harper & Row, Trophy, 1973.
Louis, who is a mute trumpeter swan, is given a trumpet by his father.

Wilder, Laura Ingalls. *Little House on the Prairie* (and more). Illustrated by Garth Williams. New York: Harper & Row, Trophy, 1973.
Story of a pioneer family in the nineteenth century.

Additional Reading About Children and Education

Ames, Louise Bates, and Frances L. Ilg. *Your Five Year Old: Sunny and Serene.* New York: Dell, 1981.
Written by the co-directors of the Gesell Institute of Child Development, a small readable book that offers descriptions of average development and behavior of five-year-old children.

Ames, Louise Bates, and Frances L. Ilg. *Your Six Year Old: Loving and Defiant.* New York: Dell, 1981.
Descriptions of the average development and behavior of six-year-olds.

Ashton-Warner, Sylvia. *Teacher.* New York: Simon and Schuster, 1968.
A beautiful account of an inspired, innovative, and gifted teacher's experience teaching "The Little Ones" (Maori and children of English background) in New Zealand.

Bettelheim, Bruno, and Karen Zelan. *On Learning to Read: The Child's Fascination With Meaning.* New York: Knopf, 1981.
An evaluation by a respected and outspoken child psychologist of the teaching of reading in America, with heavy criticism of reading primers and their effects on young readers.

Butler, Dorothy, and **Marie Clay.** *Reading Begins at Home: Preparing Young Children for Reading Before They Go to School.* Portsmouth, N.H.: Heinemann, 1982.
A small, easy-to-read book that tells parents how to prepare children at home for learning to read when they go to school.

Calkins, Lucy. *Lessons From a Child.* Portsmouth, N.H.: Heinemann, 1983.
A sensitive observation of young children learning to write about the things that mean the most to them.

Chall, Jeanne. *Learning to Read: The Great Debate.* New York: McGraw-Hill, 1967.
A classic compendium of the research on the teaching of reading, by a sane and wise teacher.

Clarke, Louise. *Can't Read, Can't Write, Can't Talk too Good Either: How to Recognize and Overcome Dyslexia in Your Child.* New York: Penguin, 1974.
A modern-day classic—the touching story of the personal struggle of a mother to understand her son's learning disability and find him the help he needs.

Commission on Reading. *Becoming a Nation of Readers.* Washington, D.C.: The National Institute of Education, 1985.
The foremost contemporary statement of desirable practices in the teaching of reading.

Copeland, Richard W. *How Children Learn Mathematics: Teaching Implications of Piaget's Research.* New York: Macmillan, 1984.
With its foundation in Piaget's research, an intelligent explanation of the way children learn mathematics.

Elkind, David. *The Hurried Child: Growing Up Too Fast Too Soon.* Reading, Mass.: Addison-Wesley, 1981.
A child psychologist suggests that today's children are experiencing stress because they are being hurried through

their childhood by the schools, the media, their parents, and society in general.

Flesch, Rudolf. *Why Johnny Can't Read and What You Can Do About It.* New York: Harper & Row, 1966.

Written in 1955, the original attack on the look-say method of teaching reading with a plea for an emphasis on phonics.

Flesch, Rudolf. *Why Johnny Still Can't Read—A New Look at the Scandal of Our Schools.* New York: Harper & Row, 1981.
A continued argument for reading programs that emphasize phonics.

Goodlad, John. *A Place Called School: Prospects for the Future.* New York: McGraw-Hill, 1984.
Result of an eight-year research project on the current state of schooling in the United States. A valuable insight into current educational practices in American public schools.

Gross, Beatrice, and **Ronald Gross,** eds. *The Great School Debate: Which Way for American Education?* New York: Simon and Schuster, 1985.
Excellent anthology of current reform movement. Includes excerpts from important reports and studies, as well as essays by leading American educators, scholars of child development, and students.

Hirsch, Elisabeth. *The Block Book.* Washington, D.C.: National Association for the Education of Young Children, 1984.
A well-done explanation of how block-building activities provide young children with opportunities to solve problems, gain insights, and interact socially.

Macmillan Very First Dictionary. New York: Macmillan, 1982.
Wonderful illustrations introduce the preschooler and the primary child to the world of words. More than 500 entries. A valuable resource for parent and child.

Moore, Linda Perigo. *Does This Mean My Kid's a Genius? How to Identify, Educate, Motivate and Live with the Gifted Child.* New York: Plume, 1982.
A practical and intelligent guide about life at home and at school for parents who think they have a gifted child.

National Commission on Excellence in Education. *A Nation at Risk: The Full Account,* May 1983.
Prestigious panel appointed by the U.S. Secretary of Education reports on the weakness of American schools and makes suggestions for improvement.

Osman, Betty. *Learning Disabilities: A Family Affair.* New York: Random House, 1979.
A common sense approach to the problems faced by learning disabled children and their families. Written by an educational specialist who has had extensive experience with learning disabled children.

Papert, Seymour. *Mindstorms: Children, Computers and Powerful Ideas.* New York: Basic, 1982.
A classic on computers and children by the developer of LOGO, a computer language for young children.

Pulaski, Mary Ann. *Understanding Piaget: An Introduction to Children's Cognitive Development.* New York: Harper & Row, 1980.
A lucid presentation of Piaget's theories about cognitive development.

Rioux, William. *You Can Improve Your Children's School: Practical Answers to Questions Parents Ask Most About Their Public Schools.* New York: Simon and Schuster, 1980.
More than 200 answers to the questions parents have about their children's schools. Includes questions and answers about school records, textbooks, school board decisions, and other educational topics.

Schimmel, David, and **Fischer, Louis.** *The Rights of Parents in the Education of Their Children.* Columbia, Md.: National Committee for Citizens in Education, 1977.

A clear presentation of parents' legal rights concerning the education of their children.

U.S. Department of Education. *What Works: Research About Teaching and Learning,* Washington, D.C., 1986.

Free from the Department of Education, a brief summary of research findings about a multitude of educational issues, including topics like phonics, reading to children, independent reading, discipline, and storytelling.

Index